TIPS

THE SERVER'S GUIDE TO BRINGING HOME THE BACON

THE CUSTOMER SPEAKS TO EVERY WAITER, WAITRESS,
AND RESTAURANT MANAGER IN AMERICA

TIPS

THE SERVER'S GUIDE TO BRINGING HOME THE BACON

THE CUSTOMER SPEAKS TO EVERY WAITER, WAITRESS, AND RESTAURANT MANAGER IN AMERICA

Make More Money!

Tricia Spencer

Illustrated By
Jamie Lee Sugarman

Lilac Bloom Press

Riverside, California

Copyright © by Tricia Spencer

Published by:
Lilac Bloom Press
Riverside, CA 92509

All rights reserved. No part of this book may be reproduced or transmitted in any form or by any means, electronic or mechanical, including photocopying, recording, or by any information storage and retrieval system without written permission from the author, except for the inclusion of brief quotations in a review.

Cover and interior art by Jamie Lee Sugarman
Cover and book design by Jonathan Gullery

Printed in the United States of America

First Printing April 2002
Second Printing, October 2006

ISBN 10: 0-9715098-0-8 (pbk.)
ISBN 13: 978-0-9715098-0-1

www.tips.lilacbloompress.com

*This book is dedicated to the customers who have suffered
at the hands of unskilled and uncaring servers.*

*And, with heartfelt gratitude, this book is dedicated
to those servers who have served with consummate grace,
caring expertise, and that extra little something
that makes them so far above and beyond the ordinary.*

*I would like to thank everyone who took the time
to thoughtfully and thoroughly complete the
food service questionnaire, for without the word of the customer,
nothing in this book would matter.*

*I would especially like to thank the publishers, authors,
editors, and agents who saw value in my work and encouraged me.*

*And, most importantly, I would like to thank my family
for never scoffing at my dreams – whatever they may be.*

TABLE OF CONTENTS

Chapter 1
Straight Talk
LET'S CHAT DOLLARS AND SENSE ……………………… 13

Beliefs …………………………………………………17
Understandings ………………………………………22

Chapter 2
Creatures
ANIMALS, INSECTS, FOWL, AND OTHER CREATURES
A SERVER DOES NOT WANT TO BE …………………………25

The Dodo Birds ……………………………………… 26
The Pack Mules ……………………………………… 31
The Snails …………………………………………… 34
The Piglets ………………………………………… 38
The Ostriches ……………………………………… 41
The Parrots ………………………………………… 45
The Skunks ………………………………………… 48
The Roadrunners …………………………………… 55
The Bulls …………………………………………… 59
The Mice …………………………………………… 67
The Cats …………………………………………… 73
The Sloths ………………………………………… 80
The Roaches ………………………………………… 87
The Lambs ………………………………………… 91

Chapter 3
Be Wise
ORGANIZE, CATEGORIZE, ITEMIZE 97

Getting The Rhythm 101
Organization Exercise 102

Chapter 4
I Spy
... ... 107

Chapter 5
Q & A
QUESTIONS AND ANSWERS, AND, . . .SURPRISES? 113

Food Service Questionnaire 115

Chapter 6
Dear Diary
PERSONAL, PRIVATE AND PROSPEROUS! 179

Server Personal Record 182
Server Diary Daily Log 183

Chapter 7
Quickies
MAGICAL MONEY MOTIVATORS! 185

Dapper Dialogue 186
Condiment Caboodle 187
Water, Water Everywhere
   And Nary A Drop To Drink 189
Shine, Underline, Shine 190
Check It Out 191
Go With It 192
Comfort Zone 194
Your Majesty 196
With This Ring I Thee Wed 198
Butlers — Talk The Talk —
Walk The Walk 200

Chapter 8
Deep Bottom 203

Leader Of The Pack 204
Smack Dab Bottom 204
Tips Scale Of Success 206

Chapter 9
Fabulous Encore! 209

Server's Creed 211

Chapter One

STRAIGHT TALK

Let's chat
Dollars & Sense!

"Call Brinks! I've made a killing at the tables!"

An excited shout from a lucky Las Vegas gambler? No way! With a little spit and polish, this gleeful exultation can be *yours* at the end of your food serving shift. This book will enable you to hit the tips jackpot if you will merely absorb and apply the simple but oh-so-valuable information contained between these covers. Why is it so valuable? That's easy. It's because the advice and suggestions you will hear come from the most important people in your financial lives — your customers.

Let's begin on a first name basis. My name is Tricia. You can tell me yours later when we meet someday where the roads come together. Or perhaps you will drop me a line. After reading this book, you may feel the need to yell at me, inform me, correct me, or, hopefully, agree with me about the points and ideas expressed here. Whatever the circumstances, I will be delighted to hear from you.

My purpose in writing this book is satisfaction — for you, and for your customers. Life is richer when we are all completely and joyfully satisfied. That ultimate satisfaction is only possible when all aspects of our lives run smoothly. Your food service job can be very, *very* satisfying. Your customer's dining experience can be equally satisfying. All it takes is desire and implementation on your part.

I am someone who understands the trials and tribulations of food service. From that understanding springs the desire to see you make as much money as you possibly can while employed as a food server. More money will certainly feel satisfying; won't it? Food service is often a tough, thankless, and lousy-paying job, but it simply doesn't have to be that way. This book has a simple goal: **Colossal Tips!** It is my hope that through this one-way conversation (I'll talk, you listen) you will find helpful ideas that will enable you to enjoy your job more and improve your tips. Bottom line? You will **MAKE MORE MONEY!** That's the plan in a nutshell. The talk will be straightforward. If I step on some toes, forgive my bluntness; but bear in mind that the comments, observations, and advice I share with you, is from the heart — the hearts of your customers. In addition to being a tad blunt, I may repeat myself from time to time; and you should know that I do it intentionally (well mostly). I *do* believe in the power of repetition. Repetition is one of the key elements of success of any kind. Repetition is the primary foundation for recall. Since this book is about successful money-making in food service, repetition serves our purposes very nicely.

Now, before you say, "Well who are *you* to tell *me* how to do *my* job?!", permit me to take a moment and toot my own horn, or spill my own guts, as the case may be. Some of what I will relate to you in this book is based on experience, some on research, and a dab or two on inspiration.

I have been a server in a broad variety of food service establishments — from a hamburger stand at the county fair, to roadside diners and pancake houses, to fine dining restaurants where there is one head server for a table and every course has its own specialized server. I have even been a singing waitress (what a fun job!). Those years of experience do account for part of my qualifications to write this book. However, the **most important** qualification is that for virtually all of my adult life, (without getting personal, let's just say, for at least twenty years, or so), I have dined out nearly every day. On a great number of those days, I purchased more than one meal a day. That's a lot of meals! I have dined in restaurants in the north, south, east, and west of our country (and a few foreign locales we won't discuss). The establishments represented every conceivable type of dining situation, from "holes-in-the-wall" to "you-wish-you-could-afford-this-place" facilities. I've seen it all. I've seen it through the eyes of a server, but more importantly, through the eyes of a customer. From time to time, I will share with you some experiences I have had and some servers I have known. Believe me, some of them were doozies! Additionally, as a prelude to writing this book, I conducted what felt like a 'bazillion' hours of interviews and research and compilation of questionnaires completed by a cross section of customers nationwide. What they had to say may delight, surprise, or dismay you; but it will definitely *enlighten* you.

Often I have seen a server struggle, run their legs down to nubs, carry enough plates and dishes to be affectionately called a barge, and return to the table to find little or nothing to show for their

Herculean efforts. What was wrong here? Were the customers just stingy? Were they just bad people? Were they "the type that will stiff you no matter what you do"? Well, sadly, most of the time, those excuses are just that — excuses. The majority of the customers enter into the dining experience with the expectation of tipping for the service. It is a surprise to all when a server has run themselves ragged and the customer is still unhappy enough to reduce the tip or leave none at all. What happened?

In this book, we will examine the most prevalent reasons for puny tips. We will look at some of the worst offenders in food service and quickly pick apart the problems they represent. We'll examine winning, workable solutions that will eliminate those problems forever. **This book is not about restaurant policy or procedure. It's about what you can personally do to make more money, be happier in your job, and ultimately, be the best you can be at what you do.** No, this is not the Army, but the Army said a darn good thing when it said "Be All That You Can Be". That powerful phrase describes a dynamite philosophy to live by, and work by — at any job — in any endeavor.

Within these pages, we will not discuss topics like whether or not it is acceptable to leave the check on the table at the time you serve the food. *Those* types of issues are relevant to *where* you work and to your workplace's company policy. At a truck-stop, such practice is accepted (even though I personally find it rude and inappropriate at any establishment), while at "Chez Whoever", it would be considered an insult and be taboo. Checks do, after all, denote *dismissal*. However, in such matters, you must do whatever your management mandates — regardless of your own personal views. Management does sometime dictate bad policy; but bad or good, you are expected to follow the policy. It is never wise to defy management. If you don't agree with management's serving rules, simply move on to a facility that is more in line with your own philosophies.

There are fine procedural manuals in existence for professional waiters and waitresses. With these manuals you may learn how to fold a napkin, write a check, the rudiments of sidework, how to handle liquors and wines, credit card processing, definitions of restaurant lingo, etc. — all the nuts and bolts stuff. I wholeheartedly suggest you read a few of these fine publications as we will not be discussing those types of issues in *this* book. Rather, we will concentrate on ways for you to impress and endear your customers. We will aim for the ultimate goal of creating a positive well-rounded server who will **make more money**. Even if you are already doing very well, I hope you will find something worthwhile within these pages. We can never know too much, or expand our horizons too far. There is something to learn in every moment in time. I want you to be the greatest food server on the planet — the one the customers repeatedly ask for, the one everyone respects and cares about, and the **one who has made the most money at the end of the shift!**

Beliefs

Society often has a disagreeable habit of 'labeling' — usually without merit. Labels can hurt us if we let them. However, we **can choose** *not* to let them. Remember this very important foundation: **no matter the action, we have the choice of the reaction.** This means we can choose to be happy, to be successful, to be at peace with ourselves, no matter what potholes we come upon in the road of life. We can soar past debilitating labels, and leave them in the dust where they belong.

Certain negative labels have long been associated with food service. Here are a few of those silly labels:

1. Food service is a **low-class** job.

2. People who work in food service are **losers who can't do anything else**.

3. Food servers are all unemployed **hopefuls of other professions**.

4. Food service is **easy**; anyone can do it; it **requires no special skills**; and it's a **mindless** job.

5. Food servers have to **work for peanuts**.

How do you feel about these labels? They're not very attractive that's for sure. What do I say? I say, **"BUNK!!"** None of these things are true, but you may be surprised at just how many people actually believe they *are* true. Even worse is the fact that many food servers themselves believe them to be true. This is an enormous problem. If you believe these labels fit you, or your job, you have already lost the game. If you feel this way, then how on earth do you expect your customers to feel differently? How do you expect them to respect and admire you enough to show their appreciation by tipping you handsomely if you have such a low opinion of your job and your own self-worth? So I say, if you have ever believed one or all of these labels, **"Stop it and stop it now!"**

It is imperative that you feel good about what you are doing. I was a food server because I loved it. That belief alone was responsible for the fact that I always had one of the highest tip totals at the end of my shift. If you love what you do, you are better at it - guaranteed. Because of that love for your job, you will care more; and caring is key. You will apply yourself to a greater degree and perform the best you know how. Caring actions translate to better tips. (And you can't fool me, I know you care about making more money, or you wouldn't have read this far!)

So let's take a look at those horribly negative labels we mentioned and dig the truth right out of them.

1. *Food service is a low-class job.*

HA! This is just simply untrue. There are food servers in this country who make more money than many so-called 'upwardly mobile' professionals (you know, the kind who are trapped in high-stress rat races). It is a job that requires integrity and commitment. There can be nothing low-class about that. There is no greater reward in life than to feel the self-satisfaction and joy associated with helping another. As a food server, if you look at it with open eyes, you will see that you are given the opportunity to do just that, a hundred times a shift. It is a personally rewarding occupation. The Golden Rule, as in everything, holds true here — "Do Unto Others As You Would Have Them Do Unto You". If you truly care about the people you serve, they will care about you. As a bonus, **your tips will improve.**

2. *People who work in food service are losers who can't do anything else.*

False, false, false! You've got to be kidding. I am educated, intuitive, talented and other great things (modesty notwithstanding) and I *chose* to be a food server. I did not do it because I was unable do anything else. I am fully aware that I can do anything I set my mind to, but being a food server provides too many positives to ignore. It's active, fast-paced, lucrative, and most importantly for me, liberating. Due to the fact that you can "leave your work at the office" when you go home after your shift, your mind is free to pursue all of the other pleasures of life.

While I was a food server, I had the freedom to write music, study, perform, and play life's games to my heart's content. My food serving jobs paid for it all. Delightfully, the real kicker was this: while I was at my job, I loved it! I enjoyed the challenge of striving to be the best server on the premises, meeting tons of interesting people, and counting my money at the end of my shift!

Why am I not still a food server? Well, for me, life just has too many delicious options to do one thing forever. Now, don't misunderstand. I do not feel that people who choose to have only one career in life are wrong in the way they feel; I just know it is not right for me. I want to explore lots of different avenues. Twists and turns, that's what I like. For me, variety is truly the spice of life. But that philosophy never kept me from giving one hundred and ten percent to my food service jobs throughout the years. I feel strongly that my dedication to being the best at whatever I choose to do in life is the cornerstone of my personal success. I do not believe that being a food server deserves less attention than being anything else. It is an honest and extremely valued profession. Food service has been in existence for thousands of years and is unlikely to ever be eliminated. Unlike some occupations that become obsolete in the face of growing technology, food service has tremendous job security!

3. *Food servers are all unemployed hopefuls of other professions.*

Balderdash! Many very fine people are career food servers. And why not? There are gobs of jobs I can think of that are less desirable. Many of those are jobs most people 'label' as outstanding and impressive. Those who think that way just can't see the forest for the trees.

It doesn't take a genius to realize that success comes from within, not from without. I was a very successful food server. There are many doctors, engineers, etc., who will never be *truly* successful in their own eyes. One of the reasons for that result is that they have 'labeled' success to be something out of their immediate reach — like multi-millionaire status, god-like power, a private island, etc. They strive and strive and strive and strive while life marches on. Success is internal; it belongs to each of us in a different way. For me, success is not about how much money I make, or what kind of house I live in, or the car I drive, or how many people I get to boss around. It's about knowing I have done the best I possibly can, at whatever career I pursued. It's about going to sleep at night proud of my actions of that day.

Tips are *one* barometer of success for food servers. I find it funny indeed to hear food service referred to as a 'job' while being a stockbroker is a 'career'. The dictionary tells us that 'career' means: "a chosen pursuit; life work; success in one's profession". If a person chooses to be a food server, and is successful at it; then if that's not a career, I don't know what is.

Career, or job — what you call it doesn't matter. It's all the same in the bank account!

4. Food service is easy, anyone can do it; it requires no special skills; and it's a mindless job.

Oh boy, now there's a boldfaced bunch of lies if I ever heard any! Being an effective food server is a challenge that requires a multitude of skills, accomplishments, and behaviors. It requires organization, efficiency, the ability to do many things at once, public relations skills, physical fitness, dexterity, intuition, strength, tenacity, and a host of other attributes too lengthy to list.

Many jobs require only one function or one thought process. Not so for food servers. Food servers must be able to do it all. Every day is different in some way. There are literally millions of people in this country who would never be able to do the job with any degree of success. If you are a terrific food server, you can count yourself among a very elite group of truly impressive professionals.

To think, for even one moment, that food service requires no special skills is a great joke. I'd like to see *my* accountant try to serve a party of eight! (Maybe for one of those home-video TV shows!) But seriously, if you are already a server, you are fully aware of the talents and efforts required, each and every day. This profession requires solid unique abilities. To ever let anyone say otherwise is an injustice, and not to be abided.

5. Food servers work for peanuts.

Now HERE is the biggest untruth of all! There is **FANTASTIC** money to be made as a food server.

Very few professions are so clearly based on performance. A job based on performance is controlled by the performer. That's **YOU**! This provides fertile ground to make as much as you are willing to make. You don't work for a fixed rate salary. Some professions are locked in, but **you** are not. You have **the ability,** and more importantly, **the opportunity,** to make **as much as your imagination can conceive!** Every single table served should be treated as an investment. You will invest your efforts to the best of your ability. By doing so, you will reap the highest level of rewards available from that table. And believe me, there is a broad range of tips just ripe for the picking!

Now I know some naysayers will whine that people are going to tip a certain percentage no matter what, so why bother to knock yourself out. Well, all I can tell you is that if you put any stock in such a philosophy, you don't have a dreamer's chance of making the most money available to you. That statement is undeniably false. Granted, there are some people (a **very itsy, bitsy, teeny, weeny** percentage) who would not tip according to performance if you served the food balanced on one foot while singing the national anthem and giving them a backrub at the same time. But, you must remember that those people make up only an **insignificant** percentage of the dining-out public. Do not pattern *your* actions on the actions of *those* people! It is the worst imaginable reaction to their actions; and, most importantly, it is a financially-fatal mistake!

Understandings

"The job is for me."

Being a food server is no different than being a rocket scientist, a doctor, a teacher, or a practitioner of any other profession. As in all endeavors, the value received rests on whether or not you are willing to give your all. Your efforts equal your degree of success. You must feel good about what you are doing, take pride in your performance, and believe in the results. You must adopt this philosophy even if you consider your job as a food server to be only a stepping stone to your future.

It is never acceptable to look upon any labor as not being worth the time to do it right — to the *best* of your ability. Your success as a food server will be indicative of your future life successes as well; don't make the mistake of thinking that it won't. Poor work habits do not improve themselves just because the profession changes faces. Whether your job as a food server is temporary, or it's your chosen life's career, you will benefit most by **accepting responsibility** for your performance and the resulting amount of tips that you will make.

"Tipping is optional."

Let's talk about the truth of tipping. What is the purpose of a tip, or gratuity? In times gone by, tips represented a person's desire to motivate their server "To Insure Promptness". They were customarily given *before* dining as an incentive for good service. As the dining-out experience evolved, tips found their way to the end of the meal and were representative of the service actually received. In our present society, gratuities are given to people in service-related occupations for **special** service given — the type of service that is **above** and **beyond** the call of duty. As a food server, you may already receive tips from ninety-five percent, or so, of your customers. Because of this behavior on the part of your customers, you may have the mistaken impression that tips are "owed" to you merely because you serve the food to the table. **WRONG! WRONG! WRONG!**

Tips are not *owed*, under any circumstances. When the consumer goes out to dine, they must pay the menu-asking price for their meal.

That price includes the food *and* having it served to them efficiently, gracefully, and expertly. They have **the right** to expect the food to be good, hot or cold as appropriate, and to the specifications that is was ordered, *without* any unpleasant surprises. And, (this is the important part where you are concerned), they have **the right** to a server who understands their job and is good at it. **They do not have to pay extra for it.**

You are not paid to do an 'okay' job; you are paid to do a 'good' job. It is going ***beyond*** the standard best that brings deserved rewards such as wonderfully large tips.

The bottom line is this: if you want to make **fantastic** money being a food server, you must **deserve** it; you must **earn** it; you must **believe** that you can. There is a great deal of money to be made as a food server, and the more you make, the better it is for all concerned — you, the establishment you work for, and, your customers. It becomes the American ideal — a "win-win" situation.

"I'm the best of the best!"

Yes. You *can* be the best of the best. How? By eliminating all bad behaviors and cultivating all exceptional behaviors. You do this in four easy steps:

1. **Recognize** the bad behavior.
2. **Understand** the bad behavior.
3. **Overcome** the bad behavior.
4. **Replace** the bad behavior with exceptional behavior.

Your customers are very concerned about certain negative behaviors. In the next chapter we are going to take an in-depth look at the acts that cause so much consternation. It's important we all recognize and understand *why* these things are *so offensive* to customers. If we do not first understand why something needs to be changed, it is harder for us to actually do the changing. We'll begin by taking a look at some server "no-no's". Then we'll focus on ways to avoid committing those "no-no's". Ultimately, we will formulate concrete ways to make you the best at what you are *right now* — a food server.

As we proceed, remember this fundamental truth: **all tips are not created equal.**

Chapter Two

CREATURES

ANIMALS, INSECTS, FOWL AND OTHER CREATURES
A SERVER DOES NOT WANT TO BE. . .

THE DODO BIRDS — *CONFUSED, AT A LOSS FOR ANSWERS, CAN'T REMEMBER WHO GOT WHAT, WHAT THEY WERE SUPPOSED TO BE DOING, WHY THEY ARE HERE —*

COMMON SYMPTOM: *THEY FREQUENTLY ASK THE QUESTION, "OKAY, WHO GETS THE. . .?" EVEN WHEN THERE ARE ONLY TWO PEOPLE BEING SERVED AT A TABLE*

OVERCOMING THE DODO BIRD SYNDROME

"What a dodo!!" Boy, you sure don't want to hear *this* exclamation from your customers. Well, good news; you don't have to!

Customers don't fancy having a server who seems to be confused and lost. They hate to have the misfortune of being served by a server who does not know their restaurant's policies or its menu. It's imperative that you have intimate familiarity with all policies and procedures relevant to the functions of your restaurant. This includes substitution policies; times when certain foods are (and are not) available; food preparation methods; food preparation times; and prices. What are today's specials? How much is it? What are the soups? What entrees would you recommend for someone on a dairy-restricted diet? Thorough knowledge of the menu is a must. Exceptional tips will always escape those servers who fail in this area. What's the solution to the problem? It couldn't be easier. Just do your homework. Study the menu, and ask questions of the chefs and management. Some seemingly harmless ingredients can be quite harmful to certain diners. Be prepared to competently answer their questions. You should know all there is to know about the foods you serve and the restaurant where you work. Anything less than "knowing them as well as the back of your hand" will rob you of rich rewards.

A frequent customer complaint is that the server can't seem to remember his own name. It is important to "tie a string around your finger" during your daily work. One of the ways to endear yourself to your customers is to appear to have a great memory. The operative words here are: "appear to have". The lack of a terrific memory should not hold you back. It can be very difficult to remember every item for every person at every table. But, let's face it, **that is your job**. It is not "service" if your customers have to do the remembering for you. Appearing at the table and interrupting the customers to inquire 'who got what' is poor service indeed. How do you remember without having to consult your customers? Simple. **Get a system; learn the system, and repeat the system.**

The key to the success of any memory system is repetition. Do it the same way — over, and over, and over, and over, and over, and over.

For example, an easy memory system for a table of up to six, is the "royal flush". If you're not a poker player, the "royal flush" is the absolute best hand in the world to get. (The mere sight of it sends me into a quiver!) It consists of the top five cards of the deck, all in the same suit, such as the "Ten" through the "Ace" of 'hearts'. In Las Vegas, the "royal flush" can make you a bundle. In the food service game, the "royal flush" can help you make a bundle of fat tips.

Here's how it works. Prepare for your shift by **pre-designating** seating arrangements for your station. For each table or booth in your station, select one seat to be the "Ace" chair. During your entire shift, **that seat**, and whoever occupies it, will be the "Ace". Now, starting at that seat's left, move around the table naming the seats as the **"King"**, **"Queen"**, **"Jack"**, **"Ten"**, and the sixth seat will be, the **"Wildcard"**. Once you repeat this behavior several times, it will become habit. Habits are performed subconsciously, and, in an instant — just as they should be. This habit can make you richer. **The people in your station will change, but the seats will be constant.** Trying to remember new faces is a great deal more difficult than remembering chairs.

As you write the food order, by each person's requests, you will place the first letter of their seat designation. For example, your "King" wants a side of tomatoes with his dinner. On your order sheet, jot down a **"K"** (for "King") next to his entree order, and a **"K"** next to the side of tomatoes. Your "Wildcard" wants extra pickles; put a **"W"** by those pickles. Your Queen and your Jack choose the same dinner, but the Queen wants no gravy, put a **"Q"** by that 'no gravy' notation. Is this easy or what? It may be exceedingly simple, but it works like a charm. Now, when you bring the food to the table, you will have consulted your order ticket, and you will place the appropriate "gravy-free" plate in front of the Queen and not the Jack. This behavior is a pleasure for all and eliminates problems before they have a chance to even become problems. Never again will you have to ask, "Who gets the _ _ _ _ _ _?" (The most tip-killing question in the business!)

If you put your designations small enough to trigger your memory, but not to confuse the cooks or cashiers, they will work wonders. I suggest putting them inside a small circle. You will simply train the cooks, and others, to ignore them. They're not for anyone but you. Co-workers will learn, out of habit, to simply ignore the little circles of designations.

Every food service establishment is different. You must develop the program that will work in *your* particular circumstance. For example, if there is limited room on your order forms, or if management thinks the cooks will get too confused (heaven forbid), or whatever the minor problem may be, then find your own method of designation. There is room *somewhere*, even if it is on the back of the ticket, or a separate companion pad all your own. The use of a simple memory system takes away the need for a photographic memory. It just makes your customers *think* you have one and that you are exceptional!

The "royal flush" is one example. The program works with any set system. Use what is comfortable for you — whether it's designation by use of the "royal flush", "Snow White and the Seven Dwarfs", or any other picture plan — just use *something*. **I don't recommend the use of numbers**, because they *do* tend to confuse the cooks. Further, they may get entwined with other numbers (like menu entree numbers), and they **simply aren't vivid enough** to accomplish what the system is meant for. As they say, "a picture is worth a thousand words". In this instance, a picture can be worth dollars and cents in the form of better tips. Our brains respond to the designation of "King" quicker than the designation of a number. "King" immediately conjures up a picture; and our brains process pictures easily. Use a picture plan! Go with what *works*!

SUMMARY*: KNOW YOUR MENU.
KNOW YOUR RESTAURANT. GET A SYSTEM.
LEARN THE SYSTEM. REPEAT THE SYSTEM —
IN THE SAME WAY —
EVERY SINGLE TIME.*

BOTTOM LINE*: KNOWLEDGE AND GOOD MEMORY
= BETTER TIPS!*

TIPS

THE PACK MULES *— OVERLOADED, CAN'T GIVE SERVICE BECAUSE OF CARRYING TOO MANY PLATES, DISHES, AND CONDIMENTS AT ONE TIME —*

COMMON SYMPTOM: *THEY FREQUENTLY ASK THE QUESTION, "COULD YOU JUST GRAB THAT . . . ?", THEY HAVE A HIGH RATE OF BREAKAGE, THEY SERVE PLATES WITH FOOD ON THE BOTTOM, THEIR ARMS AND BACK ACHE EXCESSIVELY*

OVERCOMING THE PACK MULE SYNDROME

Let's send the Pack Mules out to pasture where they belong! Where is it written that 'more' is always 'better'? Yes, it *is* very important to be efficient and to get everyone served at the same time. However, dish overload is a no-no. It's sloppy, ineffective, and rude. No one awaiting their meal is happy to watch a Pack Mule approach their table. There is just something quite unappetizing about seeing someone else's plate sitting in your mashed potatoes. Do you think you've been hired to be a humanoid buffet table? Do you just ask your customers to pick off the outside dishes so that you will have a free hand to do what's left? UGH! Don't do it. It'll stink up your tips like a pile of mule — uh — stuff.

Now, if your restaurant utilizes trays, this is less of a problem. **I heartily recommend the use of trays.** They provide the ability to carry more without draping plates up and down your arms like so many layers of cow patties. Trays are cleaner. They catch spills and drips. They look impressive and more upscale. They allow total freedom of one hand (two, if you're lucky enough to have tray stands) to actually *do* the serving without asking your customers to serve themselves from your overloaded (and breaking) arms. Using trays is like having a third arm! (Now that's an anatomy change every server could benefit from!)

Note: don't use trays lazily. Never set them on the customer's table and then serve from them. That defeats the purpose, and it's downright terrible!

If your establishment does not have trays, then you must be especially careful to prioritize. Carry only what you are able to carry and still give good service. Hauling too much will reduce your service to the "grab what you can" category — that's bad. Transporting meals is easier if you are organized responsibly. Take what is appropriate, like drinks, condiments, breads (if served cold), crackers and butters, etc., to the table early. Make sure any required extras, like additional napkins or fingerbowls, are in place before arriving with the food.

When your meals come up in the kitchen, take the hot entrees first, followed by cold entrees, and side dishes. Do not take everything for one person, and nothing for someone else. Make sure everyone has something from your first trip. Make as few trips as possible so that every diner has everything he or she desires within a couple of moments. Just exercise caution; be mindful to **not** overload yourself to the point of being unable to give good service. Nobody cares that you were able to carry twenty dishes at a time. This is not Olympic plate hauling. What your customers *do* care about is receiving overall pleasant and effective service. You cannot give such service if you do not have a free hand and cannot bend at the waist.

Pack Mule behavior can be, and must be, exterminated. You can wipe out this annoying no-no easily. Apply **organization** and **preparation**. (Chapters 3 and 4 will provide you with the tools to do it!). That's all it takes. Without trays, life is tougher, but not impossible. There is never a good enough reason to be a Pack Mule. You don't want to go home with nothing to show for your laborious efforts except a scrawny pile of hay!

SUMMARY: A DELICATE BALANCE BETWEEN CARRYING AND SERVING IS A MUST.

BOTTOM LINE: ORGANIZATION AND PROPER SERVING = BETTER TIPS!

THE SNAILS — *SLOW, LETS A CUSTOMER WAIT FIVE MINUTES BETWEEN ASKING FOR SOMETHING AND GETTING IT, LETS THE FOOD GET COLD IN THE DOCKS BEFORE SERVING IT —*

COMMON SYMPTOM: *CASUAL WALK, BORED EXPRESSION, DISGRUNTLED CUSTOMERS IN STATION, FRUSTRATED HOST, AND UNUSUALLY LETHARGIC TURNOVER OF TABLES IN STATION*

OVERCOMING THE SNAIL SYNDROME

Snails get stepped on. I think it's sad. Personally, I like snails, but I don't like snail behavior in people. I'm fairly confident in speaking for all of my fellow customers when I say, *"I hate Snail servers!"*

Well, friends, this no-no is so obvious it should require no discussion. Unfortunately, there are servers who practice this no-no quite regularly, so I'm afraid we'll have to bite the bullet and talk about it. Those of you who find this behavior to be as great a sin as I do, please bear with me. (But read this section anyway. You won't be able to agree or disagree with me if you skip pages. Tsk. Tsk.)

Now I ask you, when you are in line at the movies, do you appreciate a ticket seller who moves with the speed of Tommy Turtle? When you are in the check-out lane at the supermarket, aren't you just delighted when the checker takes two minutes to scan one pack of gum? OF COURSE NOT! It is never amusing to be on the receiving end of someone's dawdling.

In food service, this seemingly minor inconvenience becomes a full-blown catastrophe. It's a tip torpedo. Nothing is more frustrating than waiting. Waiting is even more infuriating when you realize that you really would not have had to wait so long if only you had been seated in the next station over. Your customers watch people come and go at tables served by a server who is *not* a Snail, while, meanwhile, back at the ranch, they are staring forlornly at long-empty salad plates, and you and their dinner are no where to be seen. What a bummer for your poor customers. If this scenario sounds familiar, you might as well look for your tip in the toilet, because that's where it's going to be. And that is where it *should* be. If you can't move your booty, get out of the food server business. This is not an industry for the poky.

Let's review a few fundamentals. Hot food should be hot. Cold food should be cold. Iced foods should be on ice or have ice in them, whichever is appropriate. Well, temperature waits for no one. Heat lamps are a poor substitute. A cool area of the counter is a poor substitute. The only remedy for food gone awry is your efficiency and speed.

More fundamentals: it is most unpleasant to have hot food getting colder by the minute while you are waiting for its companion food to arrive. A common example is eggs and toast. Many people don't like their eggs without the toast at the same time. Eggs get cold very easily. So does toast. Shame on the server who serves the eggs and then goes back to make the toast. It's not a pleasant experience for anyone. Frankly, it's downright irritating. Don't we all have enough thorny little irritations in our everyday lives without our meals adding to them? All food that belongs together should *be* together.

If you are responsible for making toast, dressing potatoes, dishing up sides, etc., then you must learn to have those tasks accomplished within seconds of the hot entrees hitting the heat lamps from the cooks. This streamlined organization will cut down on the need to behave like a Snail.

I have had more than one chef tell me that I was one of the fastest servers out of the docks that they had ever worked with (ah. . .those were the days). Why was I so consistent in getting the food out fast? Two reasons. One: to serve cold food was simply beneath my own personal standards. And two: Organization, Organization, Organization! Once you are organized, everything else falls into place. (We'll talk more about specific organizational tools in Chapter 3.)

Even *more* fundamentals:

— the time between soup and salad should be the approximate amount of time it takes to actually eat the soup —
— between salad and entree, the time it takes to eat the salad —
— between entree and dessert and after-dinner coffee —

well, you get the picture.

Any variance from this relatively simple timetable costs you money. It affects the disposition of your customers and the all-important turnover of your tables. There is simply no other way to say it, than to just say it: *you cannot be a slow server if you want to earn great money.* Slow is unacceptable even in the finest dinner houses. There is a huge difference between being slow and being relaxed and efficient. A slow casual walk to get the steak sauce when the steak is already sitting in front of the customer is an insult. You have already failed by not automatically providing the required condiments; don't make matters worse by creeping over to get it. (This unfortunate creeping is how poor unsuspecting snails find themselves squished into oblivion.)

Understand that I am not advocating running. You know the difference. A brisk, efficient manner does more than make you better tips; it keeps you in better physical condition. Running and creeping, while opposite of each other, eventually have the same effect on your body — wearing you down before your shift is over.

Snails leave a sticky, slimy trail in the wake of their slinking. People avoid them. Act like a Snail and your customers will avoid you, too!

***SUMMARY**: ADOPT A HABIT OF WALKING SWIFTLY AND SURELY. WATCH WHERE YOU ARE GOING AND WHAT YOU ARE DOING, BUT DO IT AS EFFICIENTLY AS POSSIBLE.*

***BOTTOM LINE**: QUICK RESPONSE = BETTER TIPS!*

THE PIGLETS — *SLOPPY, FOOD-STAINED CLOTHING, HAIR UNKEMPT, FINGERNAILS DIRTY, SHOES A MESS —*

COMMON SYMPTOM: *CUSTOMERS LOOKING AT THE TABLE WHILE TALKING TO SERVER, CUSTOMERS FROWNING AT SERVER, HUNGRY DOGS AND CATS FOLLOW SERVER HOME*

OVERCOMING THE PIGLET SYNDROME

"Sooooooooo - eeeeeeeee" Hey, if your customers are tempted to get your attention using this famous pig call, you are in definite trouble! I am certain you feel this doesn't describe *you*. Let's hope not. This server no-no is *so-o-o-o* disgusting, I am always astounded when such a Piglet arrives at my table to take my order. The first thought that pops into my mind is: "Why should I care about this person when they obviously don't care about themselves?". The second thought that follows in a heartbeat is: "Grief! I hope this person doesn't touch anything I plan to eat!"

Frankly, it is beyond my comprehension how anyone can arrive at their place of work, or allow themself during their workday, to get this bad. If we are busy, we all fall apart a little. But to approach a table in a uniform or apron that has obviously not been laundered is sick. Your appearance is **VITAL** to making good tips. Take a good look! And take this ditty to heart:

> Your hair should be clean and well managed. . .
> Your fingernails trimmed and pristine. . .
> Your teeth thoroughly brushed. . .
> Your clothes pressed and clean. . .
> Your shoes unsoiled and repaired. . .
> Your freshly-scrubbed body in check. . .
> With no dirty elbows or grubby paws,
> Or ring around the neck!

Cleanliness is not only next to Godliness, in the food service business it is **the law**. Ultimately, it is the golden sunshine that nurtures those blooming tips!

It is not always possible to change your clothes or apron if there has been an unfortunate spill. But if it is possible, do it! Keeping a spare at work is a great idea. If you find this problem occurring on a regular basis, you must work on your skills so you quit slopping yourself into Piglet stage.

While there may be some forgiven circumstances of messy appearance due to an accident during your work day, there is absolutely never an acceptable excuse for coming to your job unclean in the first place. (You don't live in a sty do you?) From the top of your hairy head to the tips of your twinkle toes, you have a responsibility to look your best. It is an incredible turn-off to have a server in Piglet condition handling your food. (If you don't believe this, just wait 'til you read Chapter 5. Mercy? Your customers have none!)

If you are swamped with orders when the chili gets dumped down your leg, ask for help. Get the orders out with the help of other servers then **get cleaned up**. It is one thing to see fresh chili on a server's leg because you know it just happened, but *dried* chili is another kettle of soup altogether. Don't think for one minute your customers will feel sorry for you if they have to look at dried chili, soured milk, or catsup splats on your person.

Take an ice cube or club soda to stains as rapidly as possible. Keep bows perky and shirts tucked in. Keep your hair clean, neat, and controlled. Avoid excessive jewelry and any type of jewelry that dangles. Wear clean socks or hole-free pantyhose (keep a spare pair at work). Maintain your shoes. Wash your hands frequently. Brush off crumbs. Check your smile often. (Keeping a toothbrush and floss at work, and *using* them at breaks and after meals, is good business!) Spend ample time at home preparing for work. Come to work squeaky clean, and don't allow yourself to deteriorate into a Piglet. Oinkers may have fun in the mud, but they don't earn a good living. Piglets are basically happy with just a big pile of slop!

SUMMARY: MAKE IT A PRIORITY TO ALWAYS LOOK YOUR BEST. IF SOMETHING HAPPENS TO AFFECT YOUR APPEARANCE, REMEDY THE SITUATION AS RAPIDLY AND AS COMPLETELY AS POSSIBLE.

BOTTOM LINE: A CLEAN, WELL-GROOMED APPEARANCE = BETTER TIPS!

TIPS

THE OSTRICHES — *HIDES, IS NO WHERE TO BE FOUND WHEN THE CUSTOMER NEEDS SERVICE —*

COMMON SYMPTOM: *TABLES TURN OVER MORE SLOWLY THAN OTHER STATIONS, OTHER SERVERS ARE REPEATEDLY PICKING UP THE SLACK. HAS PLENTIFUL, YET INAPPROPRIATE, EXCUSES FOR THEIR ABSENCE, LIKE, "THE BUSBOY SHOULD HAVE DONE THAT," OR, "DUH, I DIDN'T KNOW. . ."*

OVERCOMING THE OSTRICH SYNDROME

Ostriches are big birds who can't even fly. They are beautiful but not overly bright. Their idea of safety is to hide their head in a hole and leave their enormous feathery body exposed — much to the ecstasy of their enemies. Pretty stupid. Ostrich behavior by servers isn't very smart either. Putting your head in the sand is a server no-no that could keep your tips buried right along with your head. I don't know why this type of server even bothers to show up for work. If you're not a player, get out of the game. It is your responsibility to attend to the needs and wishes of your tables for the **duration** of their meal.

It is exceedingly annoying and disheartening when your customer discovers they need or want something, and you have disappeared on a mini-vacation. It's as if you've left the premises — and the planet. Your customers can be identified as the ones with raised eyebrows who are scanning the room, jabbing their finger in the air, clearing their throats, and repeating the chorus of the "I've Been Abandoned" symphony which goes like this. . ."Um. . .Excuse Me. . .I. . .Could You. . ." etc. They desperately try to flag down a passing busperson or another server, who, for the most part, have been ignoring them in favor of attending to their own responsibilities. This is not the groundwork for a big tip.

It is not enough to just take the order, deliver the food, and then show up at the end to inquire about dessert. Worse are those servers who have disappeared and then show up to smile brightly and say good-bye (hoping a big happy smile will be the customer's last memory when they are deciding the amount of tip to be left). A winning personality is a definite plus; but it is not enough all by itself.

By the time you have shown up, the food is cold, or gone (effectively eliminating the need for whatever the customer wanted) and the customer is feeling disgruntled and cheated. And rightly so. Your customer *has* been cheated.

I can't count the number of meals I have had where the server brought the food and was never seen again throughout the forty-five minute dinner. Then suddenly, at the very end, they magically reappear with that well-worn, not-necessarily-effective, wrap-up question, "Is there anything else I can get you?" At this point, I want to jump up from the table, grab the server by the front of their uniform, and scream into their smiling face, "Are you really this stupid or is it just an act to ANNOY AND HARASS ME?!!!! Where in the blue blazes were you twenty minutes ago when I needed more iced tea?! Where were you fifteen minutes ago when the butter ran out?! WHERE WERE YOU WHEN. . .?!!!!!" This is what I would *like* to do, but, of course, I don't. Instead, I ponder, "Why does this server think they deserve one red cent?"

Abandonment is a cardinal sin in food service. If you are guilty of this no-no, you are undeserving of reward for your efforts because your efforts have been wasted. Even if you served the food with the grace and style of a swan, and you used a good memory system so that you didn't miss (even once) with everyone's order, if you then disappear and make yourself unavailable to your customers, you have failed miserably.

There are times when you must leave — like breaks ordered by management, or going home. The best solution to these circumstances is prevention. Try *not* to begin any table you cannot finish. If it is unavoidable, the next best solution is communication. **Tell** your customers what is happening, **introduce** the replacement server, and **see** to any immediate needs *before* you go. Do not turn your customers over to someone else if they have empty glasses, a pile of dirty plates in front of them, or other needs or wants. Too often I see servers who do half of the right thing when they are leaving by bringing another server over to introduce them. Unfortunately, they then fail to complete the function by not finding out at that very moment if there are needs. That in itself, is abandonment.

It is not the responsibility of the replacement server to know your customers' needs. It is *your* responsibility. You should only depart when your tables are as happy as they can be at that moment. It's a form of hiding your head in the sand to dump more responsibility onto the replacement server than you have a right to. I know you think you are deserving of the tip for that table, so you must agree that you are responsible for it, even if you are going away.

Throughout my various serving positions, I have been a part of the unusual distribution of tips from tables that have been handled by more than one server. Some of them made absolutely no sense whatsoever. Just because your name is on the ticket you should not automatically feel entitled to the tip — not if you failed your customers. If you believe that you are, then you had better hope you never find me in your station. I am a great tipper — *for great service*. I understand that tips are crucial to servers' livelihood. However, I do not tip well to servers who abandon me in any way. It is insulting. It is frustrating. It ruins what should have been a pleasurable dining experience. Don't leave your customers in the lurch, ever. Real ostriches may never overcome their foolish behavior, but Ostrich servers most certainly can!

SUMMARY: *BE ATTENTIVE AND RESPONSIVE TO YOUR CUSTOMERS' NEEDS AND WISHES THROUGHOUT THE ENTIRE MEAL. DON'T TRY TO DUMP YOUR RESPONSIBILITIES ONTO OTHERS. NEVER DISAPPEAR.*

BOTTOM LINE: *PROMPT SINCERE ATTENTION FROM BEGINNING TO END = BETTER TIPS!*

TIPS

***THE PARROTS** — MONOPOLIZES CUSTOMERS' TIME WITH EXCESSIVE AND OFTEN PERSONAL CONVERSATION, ESPECIALLY WITH HOT FOOD ON THE TABLE, A PEST —*

***COMMON SYMPTOM:** "YAKETY-YAKETY-YAK!"*

OVERCOMING THE PARROT SYNDROME

"Excuse me, Server, but is this a restaurant, for like, say, *eating*, or, did I take a wrong turn and wind up at your family reunion?!"

The above sentiment reflects how I feel when I find my dinner getting cold while I listen to my server's political opinion, or the scores from their son's little league game — for the last six seasons. What a parrot! Parrots talk when they want to talk, and you can't shut them up no matter what you do. Turn out the lights; throw a blanket over their house; leave the room. It won't work! Once they learn to talk, they think they owe the world the sound of their voice.

Where did Parrot servers who practice this annoying no-no get the idea that it was acceptable behavior? Where did they get the idea that someone who is trying to eat the gravy before it gels into a cold grease glob, really gives a fig about the topic of their chit-chat? Being friendly is an absolute must. Conversing, to an extent, is a must. But monopolizing your customers' time with excessive talking is tip assassination. Do it, and you will literally talk your tip to death.

Chatterboxes are usually very ineffective servers. They think their bubbly personality will overcome any amount of bad service they might dish out. Now, don't think for a minute I don't like bubbly personalities. I do. I **am** one. But unrestrained bubbling cannot overcome bad service and unnecessary delays.

Subjecting your customers to endless jabbering is unforgivable. It is especially painful when they are without something they want, or their food is under the heat lamps, or they are trying to eat. Even worse is when your customers need something, and they can hear (or see) you chattering away at another table, thereby ignoring their own needs.

Limited friendly conversation can go a long way toward improving your tips. Nobody likes a sourpuss server. But, like with anything, **excess use is abuse.** Keep your personal life to yourself. (Don't you know most people only like to talk about themselves anyway?). Keep the conversation light and don't ever talk about bad things, like the state of the economy, or famine, or how bad your back hurts. Downer topics will make downer customers who will leave downer tips.

Now, as with all issues, there are exceptions. As someone who eats out quite regularly, I have many favorite servers whom I care about. I enjoy hearing about aspects of their personal lives. But there is the critical difference. It is because I am a "regular" that it is permissible. Over time, I have established, through the asking of questions, that I have an interest in their lives. It is acceptable because those servers never fail to serve me well while we converse off and on. They never ignore their other customers to talk with me. They do so when it is appropriate. They do not chatter away while I am eating. Our chats preceed or follow the meal. And here is the stand-out core of this problem: *it is not possible to do this with customers you have never served before*. You have no way of knowing if they have any interest in you other than their desire for you to be a great server. They want to thoroughly enjoy their meal. Therefore, the rule of thumb should be friendly, light, casual, and, most importantly, **brief**, moments of conversation. And, for heaven's sake, don't get personal. Your personal life is — uh, what is the word I'm looking for — oh, yeah, — *personal*!

And while we are on the subject of "regulars" and chatting, remember not to cross that invisible line into *their* personal lives. Most people will eventually volunteer whatever subjects are okay for discussion; don't get nosy!

Parrots holler at the top of their little lungs. They squeak and squawk. They never shut up. That's okay for the parrots, but for servers, that behavior is for the birds!

SUMMARY: *TALK WITH A SMILE; TREAT YOUR CUSTOMERS IN A FRIENDLY MANNER, BUT DO NOT RUN OFF AT THE MOUTH AND GET IN THE WAY OF THEIR DINING — THEY ARE THERE TO EAT!*

BOTTOM LINE: *HAPPY BUT LIMITED CONVERSATION = BETTER TIPS!*

THE SKUNKS — GOT READY FOR WORK BY DOUSING THEMSELVES IN HAIRSPRAY, PERFUME, POWDERS, MOUSSES, AND CHUNKY MAKE-UP, AND/OR, THEY DON'T BOTHER TO SHOWER FIRST, OR FRESHEN THEIR BREATH —

COMMON SYMPTOM: *ODORS THAT DRIVE RATS UNDERGROUND! THEY SMELL. THEIR SMELL LINGERS. IT CLINGS TO THE FOOD, DISHES, AND NAPKINS THEY'VE TOUCHED, AND MINGLES WITH ALL OF THE OTHER SKUNK SERVER'S SMELLS, (AND SKUNK CUSTOMERS' SMELLS), AND LEAVES CUSTOMERS COVERING THEIR MOUTH AND NOSE. PEEEEE - YOU!*

OVERCOMING THE SKUNK SYNDROME

Okay, prepare yourselves, this is a truly **horrible** server no-no. This topic stinks. I wish we didn't have to discuss it, but stinkers are everywhere! This section may scrape a few nerves, and some may be inclined to throw this book into the nearest roaring fire; but, hey, it is often the hardest thing in the world to simply look in a mirror and be honest about what you see. Or, as in this case, smell yourself and be honest about what you sniff. Believe me; it's hard for everyone.

Skunks. Boy, can they stink. Their stink lingers. It permeates everything it touches. Now I have nothing against skunks personally, not the real ones, anyway. Above all things, I believe all creatures of the earth are special, no matter the terms of their existence. Yet try to imagine eating your dinner where a mad or scared skunk is repeatedly trotting back and forth with his tail in the air, spraying to his heart's content. Could you eat your food? Well, if you could, there is only one likely explanation — your nose is disconnected. I guarantee you, though, your customers' noses are not.

Strong, clinging smells, (no matter how well-intentioned, or how unexpected), can be nauseating. There are many causes of that undesirable phenomenon. There are the obvious ones like unwashed bodies, bad breath, dirty clothes, and stale smoke residue. Then there are those that are a little less obvious, but just as deadly, like perfume, hairspray, and industrial strength deodorant. What smells worse than unwashed armpits or dirty hair? Often times, the culprits are chemicals in a bottle that have been lucratively marketed as perfume.

None of these smells have any place in food service; yet you would be surprised at how many of them we are subjected to during the dining experience. There is value in fresh scent — *dollars and cents* value. Now, you may say, "But I shower every morning and I wear powders and colognes to stave off any bad body smells." Sorry, that doesn't necessarily do the job.

What do you think most diners want to smell in a restaurant? This should be obvious. Your customers want to smell the tantalizing aroma of good food. **THEY DON'T WANT TO SMELL YOU!** This is true even if you think you smell great. In food service, (or any 'people' job) the only acceptable soaps, powders, hairsprays, etc., are the 'unscented' ones. It is beyond my comprehension that management does not simply require this as company policy since there are so many serious offenders.

Somewhere along the way, people began to believe the commercials and ads that told them that perfumes and colognes were a social "YES". Well, that is true for at least one segment of the population — the perfume manufacturers. Now, I'm not saying all perfumes and colognes are bad, (even though some of them could eat through your car battery), but I am saying that in the circumstance of being a food server, they are inappropriate, offensive, and insensitive.

A server who approaches a table wearing something strong enough to be smelled by the customers sitting at that table, is rude. . . plain and simple. You are infringing on part of what the customer came to a restaurant for — ambiance. Ambiance, in even the lowliest of restaurants, is important. The expected pleasant aroma of food is part of that ambiance. (Note: if the food doesn't make the restaurant smell good, change jobs!)

Exactly when did it become appropriate to douse yourself in manmade chemicals? Actually, it began centuries ago when people believed bathing to be detrimental to their health. They couldn't stand to smell themselves without the application of a strong floral scent (lavender was very popular). Thank the stars we've wised up to that little bit of idiocy and now practice the fine art of bathing quite regularly (well, most of us anyway). Unfortunately, some people still apply perfumes in quantities designed to obliterate any other sneaky old smell that might try to eke its way into our personal space. I am of the firm belief that some people apply their perfume with a paint roller. How else could you explain the fact that you can smell them from a block away? Sadly, this is also true of many food servers. (And men and women are equally guilty.)

Some servers smell so strongly of applied scent that you can't escape it no matter how far you turn your face away. Now multiply that by all of the different perfumes, hairsprays, and colognes on all of the different people in the restaurant, and what do you have? Chemical warfare! Who loses in warfare? Everyone!

A personal scent should be just that — personal. A hint of your cologne should be detected only when someone is extremely close to you, not from five paces. This applies if you are out on the town or on a date. As a food server, leave it **OFF**. Perfumes, colognes, scented hairsprays, and perfumed deodorants, are tip smotherers.

If I am overpowered by the skunk smell of strong perfumes, etc., I must assume the server is so self-absorbed that they are indifferent to my needs and wishes as a customer. And heaven help those poor souls who are allergic to these chemical concoctions. They can't get a meal down without having their nose clog up — totally ruining their dinner. Such agony. It's an *avoidable* agony created by insensitive (or unbelievably naive) servers who don't have a clue about what pain and suffering they are causing. You may say, "I didn't know." Well, now you do. Your strong artificial scent can actually hurt people. I'm one of them. My husband is not. Yet *neither* of us wants to smell you at our table. We want to smell the nose-teasing, lip-smacking, heart-thumping, mouth-watering aroma of good food! So many customers feel **so strongly** about this. (You'll see just *how seriously* your customers take this issue in Chapter 5.) We're being choked to death out there! Please stop.

On occasion, (and here is where some of you will start calling me unprintable names), some (not all) of the worst culprits of perfume abuse may be smokers. Smokers already have an odor issue to deal with — one they may attempt to mask with applied scent. Such attempts are unfortunately doomed to fail. Sometimes, smokers just don't realize how badly the smoke taints their hair, their breath, and their clothes. Stale smoke does smell bad.

I dare to tread on this sensitive subject because it's truly important to your ability to make the big tip bucks.

If a you are a food server who is a smoker, then you must be especially careful about how you smell. Believe me, strong perfumes are not the answer. There is nothing worse than the distasteful odor of 'layers' of different strong scents — perfume on top of smoke on top of dirty clothes on top of sweat on top of bad breath. Ugh.

Just working in a restaurant that permits smoking makes you susceptible to smelling like a smoker even if you're not. This is most unfortunate. There isn't a non-smoking person anywhere who appreciates having their food served by a smoky skunk. It is quite the turn-off. People who choose to eat in smoking sections don't mind, because let's face it, they are already accustomed to the smell. Now let's remember one extremely important point — **the majority of people in this country are NON-SMOKERS!** There is roughly only about twenty-five percent of the population who smoke. So, **if you want to make better tips**, in this regard, you should try to appeal to the majority. It's as simple as that.

As I said, it would seem to me that this whole smelly topic should not even be necessary to discuss, but unfortunately, Skunk servers, of many varieties, are everywhere. Personally, if I am approached by a server who is *any* type of skunk, I ask that they be replaced. Most people will not ask that the server be replaced. Rather, they just simply try to get out of the station as rapidly as possible and show their frustration in the amount of the tip they leave. They may never return to the restaurant if such an experience sticks in their minds. . . and, their noses.

Skunk servers are hardly ever aware of why their tips were less because they don't understand they have a problem. Well, take a big whiff. If you are, or have ever been, a skunk, open your eyes, and your nose. Remember, fresh and natural is the answer.

Let's review the **"fresh as a daisy"** laws to live by:

1. For smokers, carry a breath spray in your pocket and never fail to use it after each smoke. Wash your hands after handling tobacco products. Smoke "down-wind" to keep the smoke from settling in your hair and on your clothes. Rub your hands with lemon or orange peel to negate the smoke residue.

And remember, many view smoking as an increasingly socially-unacceptable habit — not to mention, deadly. Your customers would rather not know you have such a habit. **Never, *ever*, smoke in view of your customers.** It's true, a **few** won't care. However, the most solid principle behind successful food service is written in stone: **If you can please the 'most demanding' customer, the rest are a walk in the park.** You will reap the benefit of your attention to detail by making better tips. Nowhere is this truer, than in reference to smoking. Non-smokers are generally **more demanding**, as in *holding you to a higher standard of conduct*, than smokers. Don't make the mistake of thinking your personal habits don't matter — not if you want to make the **most money** you can. You wouldn't pick your nose in front of your customers, would you? Of course not. Exibiting *any* habit that a patron might find unpleasant can hurt your tips. Smoking on the job may just make that potentially fantastic tip go up in a puff of — oh, you know.

Now before you sign that hate mail you're writing in your head right now, let me clarify that this is not about "smoking" versus "non-smoking". I am not saying you *can't* smoke. I am saying that **if you allow your smoking to affect your presentation to your customers, your tips will suffer**. And, remember, that's what this book is about — <u>**MORE MONEY!**</u>

2. As for perfumes, hairsprays, etc., simply don't use them on the job. If you feel you just can't live without it, use just a trace amount. Test yourself by asking a family member before you leave home if they can smell you from a foot away. If they can, then you are wearing too much. The unwritten scent law for people in 'people' jobs is: **less is best!** (Effective managers make this policy — not open to interpretation.)

3. Finally, regarding the stench of unwashed bodies, hair, teeth, or clothes — if you regularly practice any of these disgusting habits, be prepared to be fired. You don't belong in food service. You are not only a skunk, you are a health hazard. It is your responsibility to practice good hygiene every day. If you are not this type of skunk, but someone you work with is, go to them and **gently** and **respectfully** express your concerns. If that doesn't work, go to management and express your concerns. This type of skunk hurts everyone. For managers, hosts, servers, bus persons, and cooks, this is a must. **Anything less than 'fresh as a daisy' is unacceptable.**

If you want your customers to become "repeat" customers, if you want them to tip you handsomely, you must absolutely pay attention to such small but important details. Your customers care, so *you* must care. Remember, skunks don't have many friends, except of course, other skunks.

SUMMARY: *YOUR PERSONAL SCENT IS VITAL TO YOUR ABILITY TO MAKE GREAT MONEY. BE CLEAN. USE UNSCENTED SOAPS, POWDERS, AND SPRAYS, AND NEVER CREATE A SMELL THAT CONFLICTS WITH THE SMELL OF FOOD. REMEMBER: ARTIFICIAL SCENTS CAN HURT MANY PEOPLE WHO ARE ALLERGIC TO CHEMICAL CONCOCTIONS. LESS IS BEST!*

BOTTOM LINE: *CLEAN, FRESH AND NATURAL = BETTER TIPS!*

TIPS

THE ROADRUNNERS — *RUNS EVERYWHERE, MOWS DOWN ANYONE IN THEIR PATH, IS CONSTANTLY GIVING OFF SIGNALS OF IMPATIENCE —*

COMMON SYMPTOM: *PEN TAPPING, SQUIRMING, LOOKING ELSEWHERE WHEN A CUSTOMER IS SPEAKING TO THEM, SWEATING, WORN-OUT SHOES*

OVERCOMING THE ROADRUNNER SYNDROME

"Beep, beep, *varoooom!*" We wish Wylie Coyote all the best in catching the perpetrator of this server no-no. Roadrunners are a menace!

I feel sorry for this type of server. They must be absolutely exhausted at the end of their shift — not to mention the fact that they have worn out a few customers along the way. Roadrunners are generally fast but ineffective food servers. They give off an air of impatience. They have more interest in speed for speed's sake alone than they have in overall efficient service. Speed alone **does not** translate to efficiency.

It is annoying to have a server screech to a halt at the table, place the pen on the ticket, and breathlessly ask "Are you ready to order?" while looking down the aisle at who-knows-what. Already, the customer has the sense of imposing on the server's day. Say bye-bye tip; because that tip is "beep-beeping" away even as you speak. Your customers do not want to feel like an interruption in your life. They want to feel that you are downright **delighted** to be serving them.

If you do not have the time to be attentive to each and every one of your customers, you are doing something wrong (most likely in the organizational department). It is imperative that each customer be allotted enough of your time and attention to make them feel as if they are your *only* customers, (even though everyone knows differently). They must be made to *feel* as if they are.

Roadrunners are a physical danger as well. Going at the speed of sound does not make good sense in food service. You must be efficient, yes, but more important is the ability to provide wonderful service. Exceptional service is that delicate balance of efficiency, public relations, and skill. If the scales are tipped too much in any one direction the service suffers. Roadrunners cause many accidents, and they can't give good service. Now, again, understand, I do not advocate walking at a ho-hum pace during your day, but going at a dead-run is worse. A brisk, alert walk is what is called for in food service — slow enough to be safe and to not give the impression of impatience, and fast enough to be efficient and effective.

A Roadrunner rarely takes the time to care about that all-important first impression or to establish a friendly rapport with their customers. They are as guilty of verbal no-no's as the Parrots. While, as we've already discussed, it is not acceptable to talk your customers to death, neither is it acceptable to appear so busy that it is a bother just having them sit in your station. **Your customers are your bottom line.** They are responsible for the money you take home. Rushing around and wearing yourself out benefits no one and often has the undesirable effect of damage to dishes, other persons, your own health and stamina, and of course, your tips.

I hate to be spoken to by a server who is looking elsewhere. Likewise for one that speaks in a clipped, impatient tone of voice. It's as if I don't really matter — as if my mere presence there is bothering them. Well, by golly by gum, if they don't give two whoops and a hallelujah about me, I reckon I don't have to care about them either — like in "Tiny tip for *YOU* Mr. Roadrunner!".

Don't make the mistake of allowing yourself to be controlled by your job. I know you are busy. I also know that it will make you happier, and richer, if you control your job instead of your job controlling you. Slow down. Get a grip on what are the most important, and what are the least important, actions in food service. Understand this; you *must* make your customers feel wanted. This is crucial to your tips.

The most effective steps to take to overcome the feeling that you need to be a Roadrunner to get the job done, are:

1. Get better organized so you can do the same procedures more efficiently.
2. Pay attention to small details, like making eye-contact with your customers when you are taking their order.
3. Speak in an upbeat, friendly manner, not with an impatient, snipped tone of voice.
4. Be consciously aware of the way you are moving around the restaurant.

Shake free of the Roadrunner syndrome. It will not help you be a great server or make great money. Instead, it will wear you down. Your job is demanding enough without you adding more pain to it. Roadrunners, be gone!

SUMMARY: *DO NOT GO SPEEDING AROUND THE RESTAURANT AS IF WITH WINGS OR WHEELS. USE YOUR FEET IN A BRISK BUT SURE MANNER AND WITH CARE AND CAUTION. SPEAK CLEARLY AND SINCERELY BUT NOT SO RAPIDLY THAT YOUR CUSTOMERS FEEL RUSHED AND UNIMPORTANT.*

BOTTOM LINE: *SWIFT BUT STEADY; BRIEF BUT SINCERE = BETTER TIPS!*

TIPS

THE BULLS — *INFLEXIBLE, HAS TO BE RIGHT, TALKS DOWN TO THE CUSTOMER, IS RUDE AND THROWS THEIR WEIGHT AROUND, STUBBORN, DOESN'T NOTIFY THE MANAGER IF THERE IS A PROBLEM AND LETS THE CUSTOMER LEAVE UNHAPPY —*

COMMON SYMPTOM*: THEIR VOCABULARY DOES NOT INCLUDE WORDS AND PHRASES LIKE: "LET ME SEE IF I CAN DO THAT FOR YOU. . .", "I'M SORRY. . .", "I'D BE HAPPY TO. . .". THE CHIP ON THEIR SHOULDER IS AS BIG AS A HOUSE.*

OVERCOMING THE BULL SYNDROME

Have you ever been in the barn with a bull? They frequently have an attitude that just won't quit! They don't expect to be told what to do, and they really don't know how to take "no" for an answer when they get a bee in their bonnet about something. As someone who grew up in the country, let me tell you, tangling with a bull can be most disagreeable. Bull servers are no different.

Bull servers definitely have an attitude defect. It's a serious flaw. Were I to discover a Bull server in a restaurant that I managed, they would soon find themselves without employment. Bull servers can single-handedly ruin the restaurant's chances of making customers into 'repeat' customers. Bull servers are truly a restaurant's death blow.

Allow me to introduce you to a typical Bull server. This is one of my favorite examples of Bull server behavior. I frequent some restaurants that are 24-hour establishments. I do this specifically so that non-breakfast types of food are available to me in the morning hours. Now, in the first place, if you are serving in a 24-hour restaurant which offers a full menu *anytime*, you should already have a clue that you just might get customers who want to take advantage of that offer. I will call this Bull server Joe; because in this true instance, it was a male server.

It is nine o'clock in the morning. On the table is a tabletop sign promoting a specific dinner that states it is **"served anytime"**. The sign gives a list of what is included with the dinner — one of those options being salad. Now, I don't know what dictionary Joe uses, but the word "anytime" means to me that nine o'clock in the morning is no different than nine o'clock at night. Interestingly, I have ordered this identical meal repeatedly at this same restaurant. This is, however, my first encounter with Joe. He approaches the table with a smile and a friendly hello. (Off to a great start.) But then, when I tell him that I want the dinner described on the tabletop sign, he turns into a Bull in the blink of an eye!

Having been a food server myself, I customarily tell my server everything I want without waiting for them to drag it out of me — like the salad dressing, type of potato, etc. But before I had the opportunity to complete what I was saying, Bull server Joe rudely interrupted me, mid-sentence, to say with a disgusted sigh, "We don't have salad at this hour." The look on his face was condescending and annoyed. I just smiled and said, "Yes you do; I get it here all of the time." At this point, Joe became downright belligerent and informed me in no uncertain terms that he had been working there for many months and has never served a salad in the morning. Now, friends, I ask you, what is wrong with this picture?

To begin with, Bull server Joe flashed his attitude problem. (Frankly, I expected him to actually start snorting and pawing the ground at any moment.) Instead of mentally reviewing the facts at hand (the 24-hour restaurant; the tabletop sign; the fact that I told him that I had gotten a salad in the morning there many times), he **assumed** (a loaded and dangerous practice) that he was right. He did not, for a moment, consider that the customer might be right. (Hey! I think I'm always right! Just like everybody else.)

Secondly, Joe was uncooperative in addressing my wishes. What if he *had* been right? (Which, of course, he was not.) Even then, he should have been as gentle and as agreeable as possible. Both of us believed ourselves to be right. **Never,** and I mean **NEVER** argue with a customer, especially if, like Joe, you don't know beans about the topic of discussion! It was not Joe's place to question my choices. Goodness, it's down-right scary how someone like Joe can work at a restaurant where he obviously knows nothing of their policies and procedures. Servers should not be so seriously uninformed. And, of course, restaurants should not put any server in the position of having to contradict something in writing, like the word "anytime". If a restaurant advertises "anytime", they should not expect a server to have to tell a customer that an advertised something they want is not really available. Such a policy is exceedingly bad management and it hurts the rapport between server and customer — and between customer and restaurant.

Joe's appropriate response should have been to smile and take my order as I presented it. **IF** he had doubts, it would have been acceptable to say, "I'm not sure all of the items are available at this hour, but if there's a problem, I'll come right back." Then Joe should have completed taking the orders of myself and my husband and gone on about his business. That is not what Bull server Joe did.

Joe slapped his pen on his ticket pad, looked down at me, and rudely, s-l-o-w-l-y and emphatically (as if I couldn't understand English) said, "*I can't make salad at this hour!*" At this remark, I simply looked at him and said, "Please get the manager." Joe did not even reply; he just spun on his heel and left the table. (I think I really did detect a snort at this point — *honest.*)

Grief. What has happened to the customer's feelings by this time? I was very angry. I was frustrated at the delay. I mentally calculated whether or not it would be worth ever returning to this restaurant. **There is no excuse for being rude to customers. None. Zippo. Nil. It is a sin — a BIG sin.**

The manager never came to the table. A few moments later, Joe returned carrying drinks and my salad. He did not utter one word of apology; he just plopped the items on the table none too gently and went away. My husband and I could talk of nothing else but the unbelievable behavior of this Bull server. Our meal was ruined by his actions.

After the meal was over, Bull server Joe picked up the dishes and said, "Have a nice day." Needless to say, the tip was one cent and I sought out the manager on the way out — only to discover that Joe had not even told the manager that a customer wished to see them. Unbelievable! I suggested two options to the manager. First option: pick up my check; and the next time I was in, have Bull server Joe serve me in the manner befitting any customer. Second option: weigh my repeat business (and that of other customers Joe may run off) against Joe's value to the restaurant and either retrain or fire Bull server Joe. I expressed to the manager my feeling that I shouldn't have to pay to be on the receiving end of unbelievable rudeness and stupidity. I also believe that Joe should *not* be paid for being rude and stupid. When you hurt business instead of help it, you should *pay* instead of being paid. Unfortunately, that is not likely to happen in our "don't-blame-me" society; but it *should* happen. Our society has become so accustomed to bad service that many people just accept it. That is very, very sad.

This episode should have never taken place. Sometimes Bull servers are the way they are truly out of ignorance of the right way to handle things. They have never learned any basic people skills. This type of Bull server can be salvaged. Sadly though, most of the time, Bull servers are simply arrogant, rude, and obnoxious people who have absolutely no business in the business. They need to do serious internal work before entering any service profession. People with a chip on their shoulder should not be food servers. Shoulder chips should be knocked off, pulverized and blown away!

I really don't expect too many Bull servers to actually be reading this book. (They never think they are wrong in anything or have anything to learn — they're just too dang obstinate!) Therefore, it will be up to the rest of you to root out, and either change or eliminate, any of these horrors that you work with. Bull servers not only kill their own tips, they kill **your opportunity** to serve those customers on another day. That's bad business any way you look at it. And since we all know that some managers (thank our lucky stars not the majority!) got their title from the "Doofus Mail Order University of Food Service Management", you can't always rely on them to recognize this tragedy for themselves.

In truth, if there are Bull servers working in your restaurant, it is **management** that needs to be fired! It is my personal opinion that food service managers are too often nothing more than glorified hosts, and that is a significant part of the problem. Yet you can't let management's failure to manage the restaurant properly cost you money. If you go to management to report this type of problem and it continues, or, if you are aware that customers are reporting the problem to no avail, then look for a new, better-managed place to work. I can't scream it loudly or emphatically enough: **Bull servers hurt everyone in the wallet!**

I could tell you what happened to Bull server Joe, but I don't think I will. You decide for yourself what you think should have happened. What would you have done had you been Joe's manager? What should Joe have done?

I can only remind you once again of the Golden Rule. Had you been the customer, would you have wanted to be treated as Joe treated me? No, of course not. No one wants to be treated so shabbily. Unfortunately, there are thousands of Bull servers working in food service every day. They are the first to finish their shift with a piddly amount of tips and blame the customers for it (or management, or the host, or the weather. . .)

If you cannot come to an agreement with a customer with *one* gently rendered explanation, then politely excuse yourself and seek the advice of the manager. Do not **ARGUE** with the customer! Do not **FAIL** to get the manager when there is a problem, especially if the customer has requested you do so! Do not **CONTRADICT** the customer. If your customer tells you they have had their food a certain way before, or made a specific substitution, or ordered something out of the ordinary, then **BELIEVE THEM**. Customers are not prone to lying about such things. All they want is an enjoyable meal the way they like it. If you cannot resolve the problem or feel that what the customer is asking for is unreasonable, or absolutely against policy, then as politely as possible, excuse yourself from the table with an appropriate remark.

For example, if the customer is asking to substitute something that is obviously inappropriate, (like the New York steak for the price of the Chopped Sirloin), you will certainly know there is not even a remote possibility that you are wrong in saying you can't do that. You try as graciously as possible to explain it to the customer; but they are still adamant. Simply extract yourself from the situation by saying something like, "I'm sorry, perhaps I am mistaken; could you excuse me for just a moment and allow me to verify your request with my manager?" By doing this, you are nipping a volatile situation in the bud. Your customer may be acting unreasonably, but you can't be sure. If they are that adamant about something, you must entertain the possibility that they have information you may not have. Check it out. Give them the benefit of the doubt. Talk to the manager and have the manager talk to the customer. Then, when the issue is resolved, your faultless and superior service for the rest of the meal will wipe the initial conflict from your customers' minds.

Review the actions of Bull server Joe. He thought he knew what the deal was, but he didn't. He compounded the problem by trying to exert his authority as an "experienced food server who had been there for some time". He was **flat-out wrong** on all counts. There is one very basic concept that you must absolutely accept: **the customer's business is always more valuable to the future of the restaurant than your job security**. It literally does not pay to "have to be right no matter what". Management may agree with you under certain circumstances, but no manager will sacrifice customers in order to keep a server employed. At least no *effective* manager would act in such a way.

Like with all rules, there are exceptions to this rule. If a customer is truly out of line to a server, then management is sure to consider the source and not blame the server. But you must know and accept that it rarely works the other way around. The way to have job security and to make great money is to adopt the philosophy that your customers are always right. Even if they are not, you must find a way to let them *believe* they are. Simultaneously, you must find a solution that will keep everyone involved as happy as possible. It never hurts a restaurant, or a server, to go a little out of their way to accommodate special requests. However, it can be deadly to stand on some policies and lose a customer. With the loss of that customer also goes all future tips for *all* servers at that restaurant.

It doesn't matter where you work — whether you work in a restaurant that relies on repeat neighborhood business, or one that deals only with tourists whom you will probably never see again. Your tips will be based on the execution of this basic behavior. Bull servers must be rounded up and herded out of the restaurant business. You must never exhibit Bull server tendencies if you want to make optimum tips. That's a fact. Blow-hard Bulls blow everybody's tips!

SUMMARY: *A RUDE, KNOW-IT-ALL ATTITUDE IS UNACCEPTABLE IN FOOD SERVICE. IT LITERALLY PAYS TO BE PLEASANT AND TO DO WHATEVER IT TAKES TO RESOLVE PROBLEMS AND CONFUSIONS AMICABLY. NEVER ARGUE WITH OR CONTRADICT THE CUSTOMER, OR FAIL TO INVOLVE THE MANAGER IN PROBLEMS. BE SINCERE AND COURTEOUS EVEN IF YOU FEEL THE CUSTOMER IS WRONG. BE HUMBLE. REMEMBER THAT THERE IS MORE THAN YOUR TIP AT STAKE, THERE IS YOUR VERY JOB.*

BOTTOM LINE: *SINCERE, PLEASANT, HELPFUL BEHAVIOR = BETTER TIPS!*

TIPS

THE MICE — *OVERLY QUIET, TIMID, SHY, AFRAID TO TALK. WISHES THEY WERE ANYWHERE ELSE BUT FACING THEIR CUSTOMERS —*

COMMON SYMPTOM: *WORKS THE WORST SHIFTS, TAKES THE MOST GRUFF OFF OF OTHER SERVERS, LOOKS FOR A HOLE TO HIDE IN IF A CUSTOMER IS UPSET*

OVERCOMING THE MOUSE SYNDROME

Being shy may be an acceptable trait in certain circumstances; but in food service, it is a no-no. I happen to think real mice are cute, but Mouse servers will find themselves scurrying around for not much cheese if they're not careful.

We've talked about overly-aggressive servers in several different ways. Being too introverted is an equally serious problem. Remember, this book is about making the **most money** you can while being a food server. Shyness shrinks tips. Great food servers must be absolutely comfortable in conversation. They must be outgoing enough to recommend items and answer questions. They must be confident enough to act with conviction and take control of situations as they arise.

The Mouse server is doing himself, or herself, a grave injustice. So often I have seen a Mouse server lose what could have been a lucrative tip simply because they panicked when an unfamiliar situation arose — a situation which they were unprepared to handle. It offends the customer to have a server who cannot take charge and solve problems. To be a great food server, you must be able to look people straight in the eye and talk with confidence. You must be able to assess a situation and not be hesitant to resolve it. You must not allow others to take advantage of you.

Mouse servers are usually the kindest and least authoritative servers on the premises. Because of this, other servers, especially Bull servers, are constantly taking advantage of them — utilizing phrases like, . . ."Could you just take that to. . .for me. . ." and . . ."I have to get home early, could you just do my sidework this time. . ." You know the type.

Now, there is absolutely nothing wrong with servers helping each other. In truth, it's the way it should be — the way it *must* be. I'm talking about abuse of that system. A Mouse server will be absolutely reluctant to say "no", so they end up picking up the slack of their co-workers. The undesirable result of this phenomenon is that the Mouse server becomes overloaded and is unable to give dedicated attention to their own work and customers. This nibbles away at tips. It's just simply not fair.

If you are a Mouse server, you must get over it if you want to make good tips. If it's an emotional problem, I can't advise you, other than to say "look within"; but if it's a confidence problem, there are four positive anti-Mouse steps you can take toward improvement.

First: Learn to say "no" once in a while. Saying *"No, I'm sorry I can't do that for you right now."* is sufficient. Usually, Mouse servers who do find it in themselves to say "no", aren't comfortable with such a brief answer. They frequently feel the need to elaborate with a long explanation of *why* they can't do it. OK, if you must, go ahead and give a quick explanation, then get on with your own business.

Second: Never take on more than you can handle just because you think someone might not like you if you don't. **Your first priority is to yourself, to your own customers, and to your own work.** This is not to say I want you to become a "ME" person to the exclusion of all others. ("Me" people are the source of all of the planet's ills!) What I *am* saying is that you must find an equitable balance between helping your co-workers when they *truly* need it (and not when they are just being a little lazy) and doing the best job you can for yourself. Learn to recognize the situation for what it truly is when particular co-workers are repeatedly asking you to do something for them. If someone is frequently imposing on you, *they* have a problem. Don't let **their** problem become **your** problem. Take a tip from society, and Just Say No!

Third: Learn to visualize the solution in a heartbeat. Meet a Mouse server I encountered whom I shall call Minny (no relation). Minny was a real shy and timid mouse. She barely spoke above a whisper and held her whole body in a perpetual position of submission.

Minny works in a 40's style diner that automatically serves plastic squeeze bottles of catsup and mustard with the sandwiches. When Minny brought the condiments, she set them on the table and quietly inquired, "Can I get you anything else?" As she was saying this, she was none-too-discreetly edging away from the table, looking for the safety of anywhere else. I looked at the bottles she had just placed before us and discovered the mustard bottle was smeared with catsup. There would have been no way to actually use the bottle without getting catsup on our hands. Oooy-gooey! Minny was already guilty of serving unfit condiments (which we shall specifically talk about a little later), but she added insult to injury by her response when I brought it to her attention.

I said, "Oh my, this bottle sure is a mess." Minny looked down at the bottle, made a cross between a giggle and a squeak, and promptly fled the area. She couldn't cope! She just didn't know what to do or what to say in response to a simple negative situation that had come up. Minny looked cute in her vintage outfit. She was a sweet person. She brought the food to the table. Yet, what did Minny do to *earn* a tip for service above and beyond the call of duty?

Not only did Minny *not* go above and beyond the call of duty, she failed to even provide the simplest of good service. Now, I'm sure all of you reading this know what should have happened. Minny should have: **a)** not served unfit condiments in the first place; but since she did, she should have: **b)** responded by taking responsibility for her actions. Taking responsibility does *not* include blaming the busperson or another server by saying something like, "Oh, so-and-so didn't clean this, they were supposed to. . .", etc. What should be said is a simple, "I'm sorry; I'll replace these right away.". Finally: **c)** she should have been back in a flash with an absolutely pristine set of condiments — bottles so clean, they looked brand new.

Minny didn't visualize the appropriate response. You must discipline yourself to visualize what is the **right look**, the **right way**, the **right response**. Every meal served should be as perfect as you can bodily make it. If, by an oversight or other reason, a negative situation arises, you must be able to resolve it to the customer's benefit in the blink of an eye. How do you do this?

You do it the same way you get to Carnegie Hall — practice, practice, practice! Exercise your mind. Watch your tables (and other servers' tables) for problem situations; then mentally solve the problems. One of the best methods of practicing is to do this while *you* are a customer. Look at all that happens during the service and say to yourself, "How could I improve on that?" Visualize viable alternatives. What? You say you don't eat out all that often yourself? No problem. Daydream. That's right; close your eyes for a mental workout. Picture the tables in your mind's eye. Zero in on the problems your mind has created and resolve them. Find the solutions quickly. Your brain will store these solutions very nicely for use at a later date. If thinking on your feet is not your strong point, then you must overcome that. How? You neatly stockpile a pack of solutions away in the massive amount of brain we don't even bother to use. Believe me; we have plenty of storage space! Just remember, walking away is the worst possible response. You can't expect to make good money by giving a poor performance. Not responding to a customer's remark or apparent dissatisfaction, is truly poor performance.

Fourth. Work with your mirror at home. Your mirror is your best friend — believe it or not. To build your confidence and presentation, employ your mirror as your coach. Make yourself as presentable as possible. It doesn't necessarily matter if you think you are attractive to others. What matters is that you feel good about *you*. If you look in the mirror and see something you don't like, change it! Life is about change. If you are not changing something on a fairly regular basis, you are among the walking dead. So get with it. Change your hair or shape or whatever makes you feel uncomfortable and less confident. I'm not talking plastic surgery or a hundred-pound weight loss or shaving your head. Changes don't have to be big. Little changes are just as valuable. Every change in life is not meant to be monumental; some are just meant to be gentle revisions.

Use your mirror to practice talking. Look into your own eyes and *communicate*. Really have an important conversation with yourself. If you are caught doing this by a family member who thinks you've leaked your marbles, respond to them by telling them to mind their own business! Take control. Don't be embarrassed; be **ASSERTIVE**! It will feel good. If you can't look into your own eyes, you won't be able to look into anyone else's.

Allow your mirror to guide you in your posture. Stand normally and evaluate what you see. Be completely honest. (Never, ever lie to yourself!) Does the way you hold yourself say, 'I'm confident and in control'? If not, visualize yourself as a puppet, and pull a few strings. Square your shoulders, raise your chin for a level gaze, balance your weight evenly, and relax. Relax into those positions so they become your nature. An assured stance and walk will go miles toward breaking you out of the Mouse syndrome that is so bad for your tips. As a bonus, all areas of your life will improve. There is nothing more conducive to success than a concrete sense of self-worth. Mice live their lives in hiding. Don't be a Mouse!

SUMMARY — *GET CONTROL TO MAINTAIN OPTIMUM SERVICE FOR YOUR OWN CUSTOMERS. EMPLOY THE FOUR POSITIVE ANTI-MOUSE STEPS:*

1. LEARN TO 'JUST SAY NO'

2. DON'T OVERLOAD BY LETTING OTHERS TAKE ADVANTAGE OF YOU

3. PRACTICE SOLVING PROBLEMS AND VISUALIZING SOLUTIONS

4. USE YOUR MIRROR AS YOUR COACH.

BOTTOM LINE — *CONFIDENT SPEECH AND ACTIONS WITH EFFICIENT PROBLEM-SOLVING = BETTER TIPS!*

TIPS

THE CATS — *INDEPENDENT, SNOOTY, THINKS THE WORLD OWES THEM SOMETHING, CAN BE TOO COCKY FOR WORDS AND DOWNRIGHT UNFRIENDLY AT TIMES, SHRUGS OFF BAD BEHAVIOR* —

COMMON SYMPTOM*: ALOOFNESS, CUSTOMERS SARCASTICALLY CALLING THEM 'MISS CONGENIALITY' OR 'MR. PERSONALITY' BEHIND THEIR BACKS*

OVERCOMING THE CAT SYNDROME

"Here Kitty, Kitty, Kitty" "P l e a s e, Kitty" "Where's that blasted cat?!" Sound familiar? Well if you have ever lived with a cat, chances are you've uttered these special phrases a few thousand times yourself. Now, I love cats, as I do all animals; and my cat, Dancer, is the best feline in the world as far as I'm concerned. But even Dancer is guilty of occasional, no make that frequent, bouts of snobbery. If she is comfortably reclining under a chair or in a box, I can call her till I'm the prettiest of blues and unless she deems it worthwhile to respond, she just won't. This is part of who she is, a cat. In a sense, that makes her behavior tolerable if not altogether acceptable. Those same traits in a food server (or any human in my opinion) is totally and unequivocally unacceptable. If you practice Cat behavior in food service, you may as well kiss your tips good-bye because they're headed for the litterbox.

Who wants a food server who is a snob? Who wants a food server who treats you as if you are a bother? Who wants a Cat server? No one. Cat servers give the impression they would rather spit on you than serve you. It's easy for a customer to get into a 'Catch 22' situation with Cat servers. Why does this happen? It's because Cat servers rarely recognize that they are responsible for their own problems.

A Cat server will start off the process by behaving badly and giving indifferent or poor service the first time they serve a customer. The customer will respond by tipping less than customary. The next time that customer is in the Cat's station, the Cat will give even poorer service because they think that the customer 'won't tip well anyway'. The customer responds to this 'even-worse' treatment by tipping even less. And so on, and so on. What's the real problem? It should be crystal clear. The Cat server is snobby, snooty, snippy, and spiteful — in other words, downright *catty*. Cats have created the 'Catch 22' endless circle of difficulty by their failure to realize they are the core of the problem. They don't have the aggressive, stubborn attitude problem of the Bull server. No, theirs is one of selfish, superior, unconcern. Just as bad! Both types are unforgivable in food service.

I'm going to tell you one of my favorite Cat server stories. I think this episode is an all-time winner in the field of "I Can't Believe They Did That!". The server happened to be a room service server in a very upscale hotel. I shall call her Dunderhead. Honestly, any other name is too nice for her.

My mother and I were attending a tradeshow that required a stay of eight nights. In hotel service, you begin to know the servers pretty quickly because you are there for the majority of meals. Still, we had never met Dunderhead, even though we had already been there five days when this episode happened.

It is our habit to utilize room service for breakfast. Doing so allows us a little more time in the mornings before going off to the tradeshow. Our breakfast was ordered to arrive no later than 7:45. By 7:55 it was ten minutes late, and I called room service to check on it's progress. The person I spoke with confirmed my order and told me that it would be up shortly. It's important that we leave the room no later than 8:40 in order to make it to the tradeshow on time. So, fifteen minutes later, at 8:10, I phoned again. I was informed the room server had our order and was on her way. At 8:20, a full forty minutes late, (and a full ten minutes after I was told she was on her way), the server arrived at the room.

As you can imagine, I was already very unhappy and feeling very rushed. What a disagreeable start to my day. Dunderhead placed the tray on the table, without bothering to unload it, and handed me the check to sign. My mother began to remove the dishes from the tray only to discover there was only one breakfast. When she mentioned this, Dunderhead, (while nonchalantly examining her fingernails), heaved a sigh and responded, "Oh, yeah, we're out of waffles, did you want to order something else?" **YOU'VE GOT TO BE KIDDING!** I couldn't believe my ears! But wait, it gets better!

I pointedly told Dunderhead there was no time left to place another order. I expressed my dismay that in two phone calls to room service, no one ever related that the waffles had flown the coop. I shared with her that during one of those calls, our order was even confirmed. With even greater emphasis, I told her that she should have checked the tray against the ticket and called me *before* she left the kitchen if there was need for a substitution. She did not offer one word of apology, but she did express her opinion of my statements with her look of "so-what". She just stood there, looking at me as if I was really an annoying flea she would just as soon flick off her sleeve, waiting for me to hand her the signed check. I handed her the *unsigned* check and told her that I would not pay for the breakfast. I suggested she discuss the problem with her manager. I further informed her that when I returned that evening, I would take it up with the manager myself.

Now are you ready for this? This is the best part. Dunderhead handed the check back to me, and cool as that proverbial cucumber, said, "But if you don't sign it and write in the tip, I won't get one." *"ARGHHHHHHHHHHH!"* If I ever felt like resorting to bodily violence with a food server, it was then. I didn't want to throw Dunderhead out the door, I wanted to pitch her out the window — and I was on the top floor!

After she flounced out of the room, mumbling unmentionables under her breath, I looked at my Mom and we both collapsed in a fit of laughter. (Bless my Mom who gifted me with the ability to look at life with humor and *patience*!) The situation was so absurd that it seemed unreal! Now I ask you, what planet did Dunderhead come from? Needless to say, I didn't pay for that breakfast, or any other breakfast there. The hotel manager was as shocked as I was and bought us breakfast for the next three mornings. One thing is for sure; I will never, *ever*, forget Dunderhead. It is unlikely I will ever see her again. I still go to the hotel, but Dunderhead doesn't work there anymore. Gee, I wonder why.

Cat servers who knowingly remain Cat servers are losers in food service. Dunderhead obviously didn't know what she had done wrong and even when told to her face, she couldn't recognize that her own behavior had brought about her demise. She lost not only the tip but her job. The hotel management had to jump through hoops to save the customer's business and its own reputation. If they hadn't, the customer, me, would have taken sixteen days of revenue (two eight-day trips a year) to another hotel. No establishment appreciates that kind of loss. Further, if they hadn't overcome my distress at being treated as I was, they fully understood the implications of my relating such an experience to colleagues. Now, when I relate the experience, it is with the follow-up that the hotel recognized the problem and did the right thing by me.

You must understand the far-reaching repercussions that emanate from bad service, especially bad Cat service. Because of the attitude problem of the server, such bad service is like a personal insult. If you have Cat server tendencies, you are fighting a losing battle. If you do manage to hold on to your job, you will always make less money because you deserve to make less money. You will always be considered a _ _ _ _ _ (rhymes with witch) because you are acting like one. I have been responsible for more than one Cat server losing their jobs. Why? It's not because I go out looking for people I'd like to see get canned. It's because I refuse to accept being treated that way. It is just plain wrong. If you have a snooty, indifferent, attitude problem, dump it. If you don't know that you have one, believe me, there are people around you who can tell you differently. *They* know if you have one. It's not something one can easily hide. Cats as animals are adorable. Cats as people are repulsive. Cats as food servers are unthinkable.

Your customers don't owe you anything you don't earn. When a customer asks for something and you bring it late with no apology for your tardiness, you are exhibiting Cat traits.

When you refill the coffee for customers who have asked for it, but then walk right past another of your tables (or anybody's table if you have the time) without refilling their coffee cups, you are exhibiting Cat traits.

If you fail to introduce yourself, or smile a genuine smile, you are acting like a Cat. If you look bored or disgusted or let your personal problems influence your behavior, what are you? CAT! CAT! CAT!

If you have a regular customer whom you have waited on many times and he or she suddenly shows up on crutches, and you fail to even ask after his or her welfare, you are the worst of Cats. I suggest getting a new line of work (the IRS might be appropriate — if they'll have you).

Now, in the unlikely event you are a Cat who honestly wishes to change, there is hope. I refer to the event as unlikely, for as I said, most Cats won't face the fact that they are Cats. However, if you *do* wish to change, if you *do* wish to make the **most money** you can make as a food server, there is only one way — thought.

You have to think about what you just did, what you are doing, and what you should be doing. Examine and review your every behavior. Look at your service and pick it apart with a fine-tooth comb. Put it under an imaginary microscope and search, search, search. Understand and accept that you can make more money, and be a better person in the bargain, if you recognize your Cat behavior and consciously strive to change it.

Begin to ask yourself questions like: "Did I greet that table in a way that made them feel **welcome** and in **good hands?**"

"Did I **apologize** to that table for forgetting their bread and did I **more than make it up to them?**"

"What could I have done or said **differently** that would have caused the customer to smile and say thank-you?"

You get the idea. It's serious self-examination that will produce positive results. Remember, every action causes a reaction. If you desire the reaction to be fatter tips, then your actions must make that happen. People tip better for better service. (The proof is in the pudding in Chapter 5!) People tip poorly for poor service. People hate Cat servers. Believe it. Accept responsibility for your own actions and change.

Get your nose out of the air.

Stop hissing and spitting.

Eat a big chunk of humble pie. Try it. The taste won't kill you. But it will definitely be good for what ails you!

SUMMARY *— DON'T COP AN ATTITUDE; SNOBBERY AND ALOOFNESS HAVE NO PLACE IN FOOD SERVICE. EXAMINE YOUR BEHAVIOR AND ELIMINATE THE THREE "I"s:*

*INDIFFERENCE,
INSINCERITY, AND
INEFFECTIVENESS*

*REMEMBER THAT EVERY ACTION
CAUSES A REACTION*

BOTTOM LINE *— FRIENDLINESS AND CARING ATTENTION
= BETTER TIPS!*

THE SLOTHS — *LAZY, LAZY, AND LAZIER STILL* —

COMMON SYMPTOMS*: PICKS UP A DROPPED FORK FROM THE FLOOR, WIPES IT ON THEIR BACKSIDE AND PUTS IT ON THE TABLE; CLEANS 'AROUND' INSTEAD OF 'UNDER'; LEAVES THE SPILLED MILK ON THE TABLE; FEELS ANGRY STARES BORING INTO THEIR BACKS*

OVERCOMING THE SLOTH SYNDROME

The sloth. He's a rather laid-back creature with not much gumption. His life is spent just hanging around. Motivation is non-existent. That's what earned him the honor of having an adjective coined after him. Our ever-reliable dictionary tells us that a sloth is not only a slow-moving arboreal (tree-living) mammal, but it goes on to tell us that "slothful" is an adjective meaning "lazy, indolent and sluggish".

These two-toed or three-toed guys are cute (to their mothers, anyway) and obviously serve a purpose on our earth. (All living things do — even you and me.) But without a doubt, their characteristics are a gigantic no-no for food servers. This really shouldn't be too difficult to grasp. Laziness is pretty much a no-no in any activity except for the very act of laziness enjoyed for its own reward — like a comforting snooze in a gently-swaying hammock strung between two trees on a balmy afternoon. There are moments in our lives when recreational laziness is absolutely called for — and positively needed. But in the work place? Never!

In some jobs, laziness would not necessarily be as recognizable as in others. For instance, a secretary can pretty much put a pile of papers on her desk and drift off into mindless numbness. Who's going to know? (Yeah, I confess. I've done this a time or two myself.) Just as long as she remembers to shuffle a paper now and then, she's covered. She can make up for her laziness at another point in time by cranking into overdrive and completing her work. Not so with food service. If you are lazy, your customers will know — *instantly*.

Sloth servers are easy to spot. They have atrocious habits. A Sloth server will be the one who will set the dishes on the edge of the table and let the customers pass them around. They will let the condiments get so low as to be virtually empty and serve them anyway. They don't ever go out of their way to be accommodating. Their primary goal is to drag out the time their customers spend at their tables just so they don't have to get new customers. They don't want to work and they let the world know it.

Meet "Slug-A-Bed". She is one of the more infamous Sloth servers

I have known. The name aptly describes where she should have remained — in bed.

My husband and I had been seated for over ten minutes when Slug-A-Bed finally graced us with her presence. Unfortunately, that was only to tell us that she'd "be right with us". No introduction; no request of drinks; no apology for the late arrival; nothing but that she'd "be right with us". I can't vouch for Slug-A-Bed's concept of "be right with us" is, but mine would have been no more than a couple of minutes more. Not so for Slug-A-Bed. Ten more minutes passed before she once again deigned to acknowledge us. As we waited for her exalted arrival, I looked around to see if there was any apparent reason for her tardiness. Her station did not appear to be full. Most of her tables were in various stages of dining litter. And yet, she would just evaporate into assorted bus stations and then be seen sauntering over to one table or another, seemingly with no real purpose. It didn't take long to absorb the picture and know that we had been incredibly unlucky. We had been seated in a Sloth server's station! Oh, woe is me.

Fortunately, we had no imminent deadlines in our lives that day, or I would have been eager to pound Slug-A-Bed into the surf for her flagrant damage to my schedule. As it was, we just waited her out and wondered why on earth she even bothered to come to work. Her behavior clearly prevented her from making any tips to speak of, and we all know that server *wages* are a real joke, so I have to ask, "Why bother, Slug-A-Bed?"

Sloth server Slug-A-Bed did finally return, but are you ready for this? Even *then*, she wasn't prepared to take our order! She merely asked us what we would like to drink, as if twenty minutes of our lives had not just been forever wasted. I was ready to dial 911 — I thought I had suddenly lost my hearing! Surely I hadn't heard her right. But old Slug-A-Bed was quite serious. I assume she thought she was doing well, because she did smile when she asked the question about the drinks. My husband informed her, instead, that we were ready to order. Her reply was a shrug and a muttered "OK" as she pulled out her pad and pen. She took the order and shuffled off like a tired old cowpoke.

The total time elapsed between being seated and actually being served something that wasn't liquid, was forty minutes. When we did finally get our food, Slug-A-Bed took her own sweet time in bringing all of the necessary sides and condiments. During our entire dining time, not one dirty dish ever left our table. This caused me to indulge in a little daydream of my own — one where at the end of the meal I would get up, and with a grand sweeping motion of my arm, I would just swoosh everything on the table to the floor — preferably on top of Slug-A-Bed. Ah, I love to dream.

I left Slug-A-Bed my customary red cent for horrid service instead of my customary generous tip for exceptional service. I do try to give every server the benefit of the doubt if at all possible. (I'm not as big an ogre as I may sound from some of the examples given in this book.) In truth, as a former food server myself, I do have built-in compassion for the labors. Not all customers are so accommodating and no customer should ever be asked to overlook bad service and tip anyway. It's just wrong.

As I left, I waited where I could see the table and watch for Slug-A-Bed to retrieve her tip. I had to roll my baby blues when I saw her go for it. I knew she really *could* move if motivated! That was the fastest pace I had seen her exhibit. Amazing, isn't it, how even the laziest Sloth on earth can move if they have a personal reason. Slug-A-Bed's reason was the tip. Now, don't we all find it extremely ironic that the one thing that Slug-A-Bed found important enough to be aggressive for, is the one thing she failed to get. Boy, was she mad, too. We watched her stomp away from our table with her big penny, mumbling to herself, with a face like a storm cloud. Very scary.

I must highlight an important distinction. **Sloth servers are not to be confused with Snail servers.** As we discussed, a Snail server is just very slow. A Sloth server is very lazy. There is a monumental difference. For example, the Snail server would have cleared the dirty dishes from the table. It would have just taken forever to get it done. The Sloth server just can't be bothered with removing the dishes at all. Their motto is: "the less I do, the less I have to do". Their attitude, and their demeanor, is very repulsive to the customers. Customers do not want to feel like a bother. Customers should never, ever, be made to feel like a bother. And customers definately don't want to be served lazily. Sloth servers should be ashamed.

I bet Slug-A-Bed can't pay her bills. I would also bet that she probably doesn't care if she does or not. Laziness seeps into everything in our lives if it is allowed to run amuck. Lazy people never care enough to do a good job. They only care enough to "get by". A "job well done" to them translates to a job simply "done". The "well" is never part of it.

You may say, "I'm not like Slug-A-Bed!" Perhaps you aren't; and then again, perhaps you are more like Slug-A-Bed than you realize. You may exhibit Sloth server characteristics but not all of the time. If you only do *some* Sloth acts, you may find that acceptable, or at least tolerable. Wrong. Any exhibition of Sloth behavior will be immediately noticed, and reacted to, by your customers. Their reaction will reflect in your tips.

Remember, customers tip generously for *exceptional* service, not service sprinkled with laziness. Don't be lazy. Take a look at your own service and honestly (never, ever lie to yourself!) critique your own actions.

Did you fail to clear a few dishes because you think "they won't care anyway"?

Did you deliver two packaged creamers to three coffee drinkers because you only had two in your pocket and you just figure that the odds are that not all will want cream with their coffee anyway?

Did you deliberately drag out the service so that the table couldn't turn over again before you were getting off?

Did you swipe a messy catsup bottle off another table, (in view of your customers, no less), so you wouldn't have to go to the bus station to get them a fresh one?

Did you serve all courses virtually together so you wouldn't have to make as many trips to the table?

Did you fill the coffee so full that there was no room for cream or stirring just so your customers wouldn't need more coffee anytime soon?

There are many, many Sloth server acts that are easy to spot. They are not minor infractions. They are *noticeable* infractions. If you look at your own behavior, you will be able to identify them. Also look at other servers, and pick up on their Sloth behaviors. If you want to make great money in food service, you must recognize and eliminate all lazy behavior.

Organized efficiency, like eliminating wasted trips, is smart behavior. Such acts are not the same thing as cutting corners off good service. Here is a simple way to recognize if an act or behavior is 'organized efficiency', (a good thing), or 'cutting corners', (a bad thing). **Question the act.** Just ask yourself, "Does this behavior **help**, or **hurt**, the **impression** I make on my customers?" If you think customers don't notice bad or lazy behaviors, even little ones, you are sadly mistaken, and your probability of making great tips is nil. By the same token, customers absolutely *do* notice good behaviors, especially behaviors above and beyond the call of duty. They expect you to perform expertly and efficiently. Lazy behaviors stand out like a sore thumb. That fact was a very startling lesson in my life.

For some years, I earned my living singing in bars and restaurants. These were my pre-band days, so I was alone. Just me, my guitar, and a microphone. Sometimes it was so hard to keep going. It felt as if the people who were enjoying their drinks or food or conversation, weren't paying any attention to me anyway. It's very much like singing in the shower — like you're all alone. Sometimes, out of boredom, I would just run some songs together, or cut some verses out of others. Imagine my surprise (and utter dismay) when patrons actually *mentioned* those things to me. You see, they were accustomed to the music being there. Subconsciously, they were even listening to the structure of the songs! If I altered known material or if I stopped playing altogether, they noticed *immediately*. It was then that I humbly learned that **people pay less attention to what is right in the world than they do to what is wrong.** Wrong acts glare and scream. Right acts subtly pass by with pleasure. It was a valuable lesson. (Albeit, a darned embarrassing one!) I share this experience with the hope that it will help you to understand how sharp your customers really are, and, prevent you from making the same mistakes I did in underestimating my audience. Your customers are *your* audience. Performing perfectly will not raise many eyebrows. It will only raise tips. Allowing lazy behaviors to invade your performance will raise a lot of eyebrows. Raised eyebrows are a bad thing. Up goes the eyebrow; down goes the tip. Customers absolutely, positively, and without fail, do notice!

Remember this. The probability of earning fantastic tips from the customers who are on the receiving end of your *great* behaviors, is terrific. You can't be great if you're lazy. You don't live in a tree. Don't act like a Sloth.

SUMMARY*: TAKE STOCK OF YOURSELF. ROUT OUT LAZY ACTS IN YOUR WORKDAY. BE CONSCIENTIOUS AND THOROUGH. CARE ENOUGH TO DO A GREAT JOB; RECOGNIZE THAT LAZINESS HURTS EVERYONE.*

BOTTOM LINE*: SINCERE, THOROUGH EFFORTS = BETTER TIPS!*

TIPS

THE ROACHES — *A COMPOSITE OF ALL UNDESIRABLE ANIMALS, FOWL, INSECTS AND OTHER CREATURES YOU DON'T WANT TO BE . . . UNPROFESSIONAL MANNER, UNORGANIZED, UNCARING APPEARANCE, UNSYMPATHETIC TO CUSTOMERS NEEDS AND WISHES, UNACCEPTABLE BEHAVIOR —*

COMMON SYMPTOM: *CAN BE HEARD BLAMING THE ESTABLISHMENT FOR 'WHATEVER' IN ORDER TO MAKE THEMSELVES LOOK BETTER. CUSTOMERS SHUDDER AS THEY WALK BY. GETS CHUMP CHANGE FOR TIPS.*

OVERCOMING THE ROACH SYNDROME

The roach, every person's desire for the perfect house guest. Right? Gee, I don't think so. The Roach server, every customer's idea of their 'dream' server. Right? Oh, you bet. As right as pickle and garlic ice cream. Yuk!

The Roach syndrome is the 'worst of the worst' of the server 'no-no's'. The Roach server is the bottom of the rung — all bad things rolled into one. It is extremely sad to know there are so many Roach servers lurking in the shadows just waiting to infect poor unsuspecting customers with a disease called "I-BOSS" (Incredibly Bad Offensive Service Syndrome). Roach servers carry this 'tip-deadly' disease because they have the attitude of a typical 'bad boss' — I'm right; I don't care about you; life sucks. How did this happen? Well, somewhere along the way, Roach servers **just stopped caring**. Because they no longer care, they adopt and employ bits and pieces of the deplorable characteristics exhibited by all other Animals, Fowl, Insects and Other Creatures we have reviewed.

As I've reiterated often, **caring** is the most important key to successful service and successful money-making. **If you don't care, don't do it!** Do something you *do* care about. "But I *can't*," you say, "This is the only job I could get right now." "I'm just doing this while I'm waiting for. . ." Hey! Quit moaning! To these types of sorrowful excuses I say, **"Get over it!"**

Because this may not be your job of choice right now is not an excuse for not caring. Because you are just trying to pay the rent is not an excuse for not caring. Because you feel you can't quit because you may not find something else is not an excuse for not caring. You see; **there are simply no valid excuses for not caring.** If you don't care about something you are spending your time doing, then you are cheating yourself out of precious heartbeats. Why?

It is so much harder on our emotional and physical well-being if we are unhappy. Being unhappy robs us of money, a sense of peace and accomplishment, and creativity. Worse, it can quite literally make us sick and steal away our most precious gift — time. Unvented stress, unhappiness and apathy hurts our bodies and our minds. But the really neat part is, we don't have to be unhappy if we don't **want** to be, or **allow** ourselves to be.

Now I know that you are saying, "Yeah, right, sure; it's easy for you to say." Well, it is easy for me to say, because I **understand** and **believe** it. That belief is not because my life has been just one big beautiful bed of roses. It hasn't. I've been to Hell and back, on a number of occasions. It's all a matter of accepting responsibility for absolutely everything that happens to you in your life. Accepting responsibility is an incredibly freeing feeling. It's like walking through a magic door to the universe because it opens up the realm of opportunity like nothing else can. Once you do that, you will cease to place blame on someone else for your shortcomings, failures, and sadness. Placing blame makes you a victim, and victims suffer. Is that what you want? Do you want to suffer? Your job as a food server is no less, or no more, important than you make it for yourself. There is plenty to like and enjoy about your job. There is plenty of money to be made. There are plenty of memories to store away for looking back. It's up to you. Happiness is not a gift; it is an achievement — an achievement that happens within ourselves, *because* of ourselves.

What could you do to encourage yourself to care more for your job? Just one thing. **Care more about yourself.** Care whether or not you are happy and healthy. Care whether or not you are good at what you do. Care whether or not you succeed in your own eyes. Don't expect anyone else to care about you if you don't care about yourself. When you care more, you will do better. When you do better, you will **make more money**. As a bonus, you will feel wonderful about yourself and your daily accomplishments. Success is not built on giant leaps; it is built on small, sturdy steps.

It is bad enough if you are one of the other 'Animals, Fowl, Insects and Other Creatures'; but if you are a Roach server, please, for the sake of us all, **FIND ANOTHER LINE OF WORK!!** Your customers don't want you, your fellow servers don't want you, your management doesn't want you, and heaven knows, I don't want you at my table! Get the hint? Choose to be happy and great, or choose to hit the road. Roaches (of the insect, or human, variety) are never a welcome sight in any restaurant!

SUMMARY: *GET WITH THE PROGRAM! LOVE IT OR LEAVE IT; LIFE IS TOO FLEETING TO WASTE PRECIOUS TIME WISHING YOU WERE SOMEWHERE ELSE.*

BOTTOM LINE: *CARING AND TAKING RESPONSIBILITY FOR THE JOB = THE JOB TAKING CARE OF YOU. . . AND OF COURSE, BIGGER TIPS!*

And now, we have one final creature to discuss in this section, and that is. . .

THE LAMBS — GETS LOST FREQUENTLY OR FOLLOWS BLINDLY WITHOUT CONSCIOUS THOUGHT —

COMMON SYMPTOM*: CAN QUOTE MOTHER GOOSE VERBATIM, "MARY HAD A LITTLE LAMB, IT'S FLEECE WAS WHITE AS SNOW, EVERYWHERE THAT MARY WENT, THE LAMB WAS SURE TO GO."*

OVERCOMING THE LAMB SYNDROME

Lambs are among the most adorable animals on earth. I could never ever contemplate eating a lamb even though I know that many people consider 'rack of lamb' to be a divine dish. It seems only natural that all creatures of the earth have the right to a normal, healthy, loving existence before being devoured by humans for no good reason other than to appease the tiniest of glands that seems to rule our world — the taste bud.

The same philosophy is true for Lamb servers. They, too, should be allowed to have a normal, healthy, loving, growing-up period, in order to be a great food server.

It is the abhorrent "Mary" system that is most responsible for creating all the bad behaviors we have discussed. It is the widely-**used** and more widely-**abused** practice of "follow me to slaughter" server training. It happens in virtually every dining establishment. A new server comes on board and they are assigned to a senior server for 'training'. Professionals may call this practice "trailing". (Well we all know what happens when we trail behind the lead dog, those in the rear get to step in the you-know-what.) Trailing is only *partially* a good thing. Why? This system does not work unless the "Mary" trainer has absolutely **not one bad behavior** to pass on to the "Lamb" trainee. Sadly, that is rarely the case. I can't count the number of times I have witnessed "Lambs" learn the bad habits and faulty methods of "Mary" servers only to suffer needlessly down the road. Then, they someday find themselves in the role of "Mary" where they pass down bad habits on top of bad habits. And it goes on, and on, and on.

Lamb servers need to learn from **all** servers, not just one. They need to train with a different server every few hours. By doing so, Lambs benefit from seeing different methods and behaviors. They can then choose what is right for them. They can discard the behaviors they recognize to be unproductive. It makes new servers more rounded and knowledgeable. New servers need to follow for half of their training and "do" for the other half. "Mary" servers often talk a good game but they have a tendency to do it all themselves and just "describe" what should or should not be done. All human beings learn better by 'doing' than by 'hearing'. I suggest your first practice table be with the manager as your customer. You may feel a tad nervous, but a responsive, caring manager is the best customer for the job. A *real* customer is by far more difficult in the long run.

New servers should also study company policy manuals **before** actual training to establish a sound knowledge base. When you are hired, ask for a company manual and a menu to take home and then pretend you are in school and study and test yourself. Do it until you know *all* you need to know about the menu and restaurant policy. When you get to the job, don't be afraid to ask questions. If your "Mary" gets annoyed with your questions, ask for another "Mary". Following meekly behind your "Mary", nodding and saying "Uh huh, uh huh", won't help you. It won't help your customers. It won't help anyone. Employing these training actions represents time well spent in the learning and growing phase of becoming an extraordinary food server. Even experienced food servers should do this in a new establishment in order to get into the rhythm of the new place.

If you are reading this book, you will have a great ally in your endeavors (if I do — ever so humbly — say so myself). Learn to recognize the classic bad behaviors and methods as well as the good ones, and choose accordingly. Remember, this book is about making **more money**. I may sound like a broken record, but it is important to remain focused on why you're investing your time reading this book. Making more money in food service is an honorable goal. I know you can make as much as you want — by caring and choosing properly. Part of that process is to choose **not** to be so caught up in the "Mary" system that you are totally molded by it. Look upon your "Mary" as *one* of *many* resources from which you will learn. Then learn enough that you will **not repeat** your "Mary's" bad behaviors or methods.

You will learn to automatically recognize those bad behaviors and methods by:

- reading this book,
- playing the "I Spy" game we will talk about later,
- becoming a conscientious 'customer' yourself,
- practicing positive personal steps,
- emulating other big-money-making servers,
- applying that ever-valuable Golden Rule, which calls for taking actions and employing methods in the service of your customers you would enjoy if you were the customer.

Lambs, sadly, are repeatedly led to slaughter, unsuspecting and innocent of "why" it's happening. Don't let this happen to you as a food server.

Remember the **"More Money"** rules of training:

The more information you have, the **more money** you will make.

The more "Mary" mentors you learn from, the **more money** you will make.

The more you mentally and physically "do", the **more money** you will make.

The more you apply all you learn, the **better you will become,** and, *THE MORE MONEY YOU WILL MAKE!*

You wouldn't be doing the job at all if you didn't need the money. (I've known very few independently wealthy persons or lotto winners who continue as food servers — or in any other job for that matter.) Therefore, if you need money in the first place, then why not make **BIG MONEY** while you're at it?! It's in your power. You can do it. If you make less than you are capable of making, you are cheating the most important person in your life — **YOU**.

SUMMARY: *LEARN FROM EVERY SOURCE AVAILABLE TO YOU; DON'T BECOME A LAMB TO ANY ONE "MARY"; BE DISCERNING AND DISCARD THE BAD HABITS YOU RECOGNIZE IN ANY "MARY" YOU SEE*

BOTTOM LINE: *WELL-ROUNDED, VARIED TRAINING = BETTER TIPS!*

Chapter Three

BE WISE

Organize, Categorize, Itemize

If I could impart to you, in just a single word, the most significant and vital element of greatness as a food server, that word would be: **Organization.**

The difference between a mediocre food server who makes mediocre tips, and an outstanding food server who is undoubtedly richer, is the level of organization that is second nature to the server. A food server who lacks complete and precise organization can never hope to make optimum money in tips. It just won't happen. Without organization, you will simply not be able to perform as well as the server who *is* organized. You will be more tired, more rattled, and more ineffective. Your customers will be less likely to become "regulars" in your station. Believe it. **Customers want to be served by someone who is organized and functions with the precision and timing of a well-oiled clock.** So how does one become organized? Easy. Use your head.

Organization is brain work. You may think of food service as basic manual labor. Don't. If you think along those lines, you are definitely short-changing yourself, your job, and your tips. It is the mind that dictates procedure. Organization can be learned and can always be improved upon. As time goes by, events take place which show you an improved way for a specific procedure to be performed with better organization. You merely have to tuck those learned methods away for future use. When you do, they will always be there for you.

In food service, organization begins with one very basic rule:

NEVER, EVER, BE EMPTY-HANDED

Commit this basic principal to your active consciousness and never allow it to slip from your mind. Act on it until your hands feel funny if there's nothing in them. If you master this one simple concept, you are well on your way to making better money. This foundational work habit gives you the edge that is so necessary to big tip success.

If you take more than a few steps with nothing in your hands, you are wasting precious energy. In food service, there is absolutely always something that needs moving from "here" to "there". Food needs to be served to the table. Dishes need to be removed from the table. Sidework needs to be completed. Stock needs to be replenished. Etc., etc., etc. The picture is clear. If you move around empty-handed, there won't be adequate time to properly serve your customers. Yet you need more than just *adequate* time. You need *ample* time to serve in a manner that is *exceptional*. **Empty hands are a tip killer.**

Don't make wasted trips. Some examples of wasted trips would be:

1. carrying one bottle of catsup to one table and then returning empty-handed to get the coffee pot for another table

2. delivering food to one table and returning to the kitchen to get food for another table, without taking used dishes back with you from any table in your station

3. taking an order from one table and returning to the kitchen, or computer, to turn it in, without checking with another of your tables to see to their needs

4. filling salt and peppers without also seeing to the sugars, creamers, or any other appropriate condiment that is a staple to your tables

Recognize the pattern. The failure to keep your hands full and busy only adds to your stress. The work must be done at some point. If you have wasted precious moments just "traveling" with idle hands, then you must go faster and work harder to accomplish the same things. **Concerning performance, your customers will be more impressed with efficient organization than anything else.** The reason for this is no mystery. It means you have taken care of their needs before they even became needs. Customers should not have to ask you to do basic serving and clearing. They should not have to sit at a table where these things do not happen automatically. Keeping a table as fresh as possible, by removing empty dishes and discarded trash, is just as important as serving the meal in the first place. Do it efficiently and discreetly and you will make a powerful impression. Anticipate their needs and you will win their respect. They will demonstrate their respect with better tips. As a bonus, you will not be nearly as worn and frazzled at the end of your shift. Nothing wears you down faster than running for items that could have gotten where they needed to be if you had just remembered to **never, ever, be empty-handed**. Keeping your hands full eliminates bother and fuss and panic.

Being organized includes anticipation. Anticipation is more than just a great Carole King song; it is one of your most valuable tools. Wielded effectively, this tool does to your tips what a helium tank does to balloons — it *inflates* them!

If someone orders iced tea, coffee, or water, it is highly probable they will consume more than one serving of it. Therefore, keeping the glass or cup full by noticing when it is *nearly* empty, and not when it is *completely* empty, is proper food server behavior. Taking the appropriate steps to correct the situation, before it is an issue, is the path to bigger tips. The uncomplicated act of replacing a little liquid can move mountains for you. It shows your customer how much you truly care about their dining experience. It makes them take notice of you in a subtle but oh-so important way. The same is true of extra napkins, a clean table, more condiments, etc. I am truly amazed at how many servers fail to notice my needs.

Did I squeeze my lemon in my first glass of iced tea? If I did, what makes you think I don't want a new lemon for my second glass of iced tea?

If I asked for extra ice to begin with, why would I suddenly enjoy my refill drink with only a few remaining cubes.

Do I have a messy dinner that will consume extra napkins? Then why aren't they automatically offered before I have to resort to wiping my hands on my shirt?

Am I finished eating and trying to find room on the table to put my newspaper? Then why haven't you noticed that my dirty dishes need removing?

Anticipation is an important aspect of organization. **Use your head to think ahead.**

Getting The Rhythm

Let's talk about achieving the rhythm of physical organization. When I speak of rhythm, I speak not only figuratively, but in reality. When I was young (...er), I was a marching member, then ultimately, an instructor, of a drum and bugle corp. One of the many positives that experience taught me was the value of precision, discipline, and cadence. Were I to contemplate walking ten miles, I would shudder with horror. I just know that at the end of such a trek, (if I make it), I will feel exhausted, my muscles will be screaming, and my feet will need a fire extinguisher. Amazingly, I could *march* that same ten miles and follow it up with a night of dancing. (Ok, Ok, I could have done so a few years ago, anyway.) Why? Rhythm. In all endeavors, we must find our most effective rhythm. Cadence and precision and discipline breathe an energy all their own that ultimately overshadows the act of movement itself. The brain is occupied. It is the brain that sends the signals to every other point in our bodies. If the brain is engaged in productive organization, our limbs will absolutely follow suit with little protest. Getting into the rhythm of your workday, through organization, precision, timing, and discipline, will make your days as a food server fly with delight. Here's an exercise to help you get the rhythm of physical organization.

Organization Exercise

Begin by collecting the following items:

- Clock or watch — one with a second hand is preferable.
- A good-sized cardboard box — one that is approximately two foot square or so.
- Numerous items to be packed into the box. The items can be any household items of various shapes and sizes. Be sure to gather plenty. You don't want to have to look for more once you have started. I suggest gathering enough to fill your couch, using no single item that is over approximately eight inches in size. Some examples of good items would be: books, dishes, utensils, medicine bottles, tools, shoes, baskets, knickknacks, bottles and jars, washcloths, etc. Just don't get too many items of the same type. It is very important that the items be diverse. Be sure to get a lot of items. Don't be lazy; you can put them back later. It's necessary that there be at least twice as many items as you think will fit into your cardboard box. You must have a broad and varied selection for the exercise; so fill that couch!

Stop reading **and** . . .

GATHER CLOCK, BOX AND ITEMS NOW!

Now that you have gathered your items, let's continue. The object is to pack the items you have gathered into the box. You will, of course, not be able to pack them all, as there are too many to fit. (You did gather a whole bunch, didn't you?) You will check the time and begin packing. Pack until the box is full to the brim. Don't overfill it. The lid must be able to close. Even if your box does not have a lid, imagine that it does, and don't pack above that line. Be prepared to record your time the second you are finished. Okay, **stop** reading, **and**. . .

CHECK YOUR TIME AND PACK THAT BOX!

Now that the box is full, note the **exact** time it took you to pack the box, then **remove** the items and count them. Write down your time and the number of items you successfully packed into the box.

How do you think you did? Did you do it in good time? Did you use a large number of items? Did you do it with no damage? Uh huh.

Now, add ten more items to those you removed from your box; check your time; and pack it again.

DO IT NOW!

Did you get the additional ten items in the box? Did your time improve? Are you using your head?

Keep repeating this process until it is *truly* not possible to add any more items. When you are finally satisfied you have done your best job of packing the box, take a final tally of the number of items and check your times. The object is to get as many items in the box as possible, in as short of time as possible, doing it carefully without any damage to any of the items. That means no cracks or breaks, no bent corners, no dents — *no damage*.

How did you do?

Between the first attempt and the last attempt a number of changes will evolve. You will begin to notice little nooks and crannies where something could be packed, that at first, perhaps weren't apparent. Then you will start to think about packing items inside other items before placing the original items in the box. Or perhaps, you ponder, if something were partially dismantled, it would take less space. But how much would the dismantling cost you in time? By examining and contemplating better methods, you are using your brain to guide your hands. Your times and number of items should improve with each attempt. Organization is *brainwork*. The hands are merely the tools that execute what the brain has resolved to be the best way of doing something.

You may be surprised, and impressed, at just how many items you can get into the box, *after* you thought there was absolutely no room for more. Why are they able to get in? Organization. Why does your time improve each time? Rhythm. If you do the exercise properly, you will eventually eliminate all the dead space in your box. Your mind will begin to look at the items themselves in a different light. You will begin to see, in the blink of an eye, which item would be best packed into a certain space. You will recognize which item would fit perfectly with another so that the two together would consume less area. You will become more aware of which physical position of each item would make for optimum packing. It is exactly the same with food service. If you eliminate the dead "space" and dead "movement" in your day, you will get more accomplished and do it faster. You will become a more effective server. You will **make more money!**

    Some servers are beautifully organized. They can serve the same party of diners in half the time it would take another, less-organized server, to do so. It is because the organized server will not allow dead space, or dead movement, in their work habit, whatsoever!

*Loading a tray is just like packing that box.

*Removing used dishes is just like packing that box.

*Serving all of your tables at once, gracefully and efficiently, is just like packing that box.

It all comes down to organization. Practice makes perfect. What a wise old saying that couldn't be truer! However, there is a pitfall to the act of practicing — practicing must be of the absolute *best* method or it can be quite damaging. Unfortunately, doing something over and over the wrong way (bad practice) has the same result as good practice. It becomes second nature. In effect, you are practicing and ingraining those bad behaviors into your everyday work life. Without fail, you must prevent that from happening. Practice makes for perfect *only* if the *method* you practice is the perfect one. Concentrate on doing it the right way, the best way. Don't settle for less than best. Force yourself to get more items into the box. Force yourself to eliminate the dead space and dead movement in your job. If you do so, soon it will be subconscious and easy. Soon you will wonder how you ever did it any other way. Soon you will be the best server in your establishment, and you will be feeling physically better at the end of your shift. And soon, you will be making **more money**!

The number of items you got into the box, and the time it took you to do it, is very telling. If you settled for, or were satisfied with, the first or second attempt, you should realize you probably need work. I didn't see your box, but I'm willing to bet that you could have gotten more in there if you had cared enough to try again. If you had thought it out, had practiced and experimented with new methods, and had not settled for second-best, I'm certain you would have experienced organizational improvement. As a food server, dead space and dead movement are your enemies. Organization is the weapon you need to defeat those enemies.

Get the rhythm through timing and cadence. Get the organization by practicing tight effective movement and placement; and **never, ever be empty-handed**!

Chapter Four

I SPY

One of the most effective methods of improving your abilities in food service is a personal game I fondly call "I Spy". Think about it. What qualities do you find in a good spy? They have patience, tenacity, incredible attention to detail, the ability to absorb the scene at a glance, and daring personality. These same 'spy' qualities can escalate your performance, and your tips, by leaps and bounds.

In most games, the object is to win. (Being a good loser is an admirable virtue, but winning is a blast!) This game of "I Spy" is no different. The object is to win by making more money in tips. The rules of the game are easy. To play, you must think like a spy.

To a spy, there is no such thing as an unimportant detail. Everything a spy sees or hears is a potential clue or bit of valuable information. He is incredibly aware of his surroundings. (For simplification, I am making our spy a he, but we all know that a 'she' makes just as wonderful a spy — or anything else.)

His eyes are ever alert. His ears are ever attuned. Those eyes and ears are his lifeline to information, in other words, the tools of his trade. If he failed to utilize his tools properly, he would fail at his job, and possibly lose his life in the process. Now a food server does not have to be concerned with loss of life. (Thank Heavens!) But they do have to be concerned with loss of *livelihood*. If food servers fail to employ every available tool at their disposal, they are cutting their own financial throat. One of the foremost tools at your disposal as a food server is the ability to think like a spy.

To train your brain to think in this manner, you will need to practice and exercise the 'ole gray matter. Stretch it; work it. The brain is not unlike any other muscle in the body. If it doesn't get used, it flabs up and dies a slow miserable death. It is amazing to me how people will go to the gym for hours and hours just to work on one particular set of muscles and never even give a thought to the control center. Brains need workouts too. A spy knows this and keeps his brain sharp. For better tips, follow his lead.

The object is to take as much in at a glance as possible, process that information, and act on it. Here's how you practice.

When you are on your own time, (for example when you are on break, or are dining out yourself), give your brain a workout by stretching your eyes and ears. First your ears.

Listen, listen, listen. Listen to your customers and to other servers' customers and to other diners and other servers. Absorb the comments as a sponge sucks up a puddle. Don't just let the noise float over you. Concentrate on it. Think about the comments you hear and wonder about them. Did you hear a customer say, "Geez, what time is it anyway, how long have we been here?" Even if they are not *your* customer, think about that comment. What prompted the customer to say it? Have they been forced to wait overlong? Is their server missing in action? Recognizing that casual comments are certain indicators of problems, *or* satisfactions, gives you a powerful tool for improving your own performance. If you overhear another server say, "Grief, that customer at table seven is a pain in the fanny!", don't accept that comment at face value. Check it out for yourself. Wander by that table if possible and try to determine for yourself why the server made that comment. Perhaps the customer isn't a pain at all. Perhaps the server is giving poor service; and when the customer has to continually ask for things, the server is interpreting that as being bothersome. The truth may be that the server brought the customer's behavior on themselves. The server's actions may have generated negative reactions. Learn from others' mistakes as well as your own. Mistakes are valuable teachers.

A good spy hears all and processes all they heard. They sift through what information is crucial and what is not. Don't tune out. Listen like a spy. As we become busy, it is common to become mentally isolated and tunnel-focused. It's easy to ignore all else that goes on around us. This is a mistake. The comments you hear are excellent tools. Practice listening. It may sound silly, but the truth is, while most of us "hear", very few of us actually "listen".

To exercise this tool you need to practice. After you have a conversation with someone, try to recall everything they said. I mean *everything*, not just the gist of the conversation. It's pretty darn hard. It requires concentration and absolute attention. Learning to apply such concentration and attention in the blink of an eye, as second nature, is the key to utilizing the tool known as your ears. If you listen to what your customers, and other server's customers say, (or don't say, as the case may be), you will have a wealth of information to process. Such valuable information will improve your performance and your tips.

Give your ears a workout. Close your eyes and listen. Depriving yourself of one of your senses often enhances others. Sit on a park bench, and close your eyes. Let your ears paint the picture in your mind that your eyes would see if they were open. Don't just listen for the sound of the birds singing, listen for the sound their wings make when they fly. Listen for the sounds their beaks make when they peck for food. Really, *really* listen. Repeat this exercise often. Do it in your car (ah. . .not when you're behind the wheel, please). Do it in your living room. Do it anywhere and everywhere. Listen for sounds you have never heard before. Sharpen your skills as a listener and use what you learn to improve your abilities.

Make your brain work. Reading exercises the brain. Problem-solving exercises the brain. Remembering exercises the brain. Listening exercises the brain. Every one of us would profit from kicking our brain in its bossy butt once in a while to get it going on the right path. Listening and recalling what you have heard does just that. It's a simple spy tool that will work for you. In the "I Spy" game, the best listeners are usually the winners.

As for developing your 'spy' eyes, you must simply **pay attention**. Again, this part of the game is played when you have a free moment during your work day or when you have gone out to dine yourself.

Look at a table, for just a few seconds, then look away and make a list of everything on the table. Don't cheat and sneak another look while you're are making your list. (Remember, never, ever lie to yourself!) I recommend physically making the list with a notepad and pen. Once your list is complete, look back at the table to see how you did. How many items did you miss?

Repeat the exercise many, many times. The more you practice, the better you will become. After many repetitions of this part of the game, begin to make it more difficult. Now, in addition to listing all of the items on the table, also plot their location on a diagram you construct. Did you remember them in their exact location? Had someone moved an item during the time you were making your list, or did you just not remember where the item was in the first place?

Let's see how you do. You see two customers at a deuce, and a table for two is an easy place to start. You glance over, concentrate for a few seconds and then make your list. Your list may look something like this:

> three glasses
> two dinner plates
> one steak knife
> four forks
> three spoons
> one knife
> one salt
> one pepper
> one carnation in a vase

That's a fairly long list for a few seconds of observation, right? Well, sorry. I'm not impressed until you can tell me what's *in* the glasses and *on* the plates, the level of salt in the shaker, and the color of the carnation. See the difference? Whatever your eyes see, they record and send that information to your brain. Therefore your brain is fully aware that two of the glasses held water and one held iced tea. One plate contained remnants of a steak and a crumpled paper napkin, while the other had bits of succotash, mashed potatoes, baked chicken and gravy (obviously a finicky eater). The salt was one-third full; and the carnation was pink. Your brain has all of this information, and much more. It is up to you to make it cough it up so that you can put all of the information on your list.

Remember when I said that a picture is worth a thousand words? (I *am* the first to have ever said that, right?) Well, when you glanced at that table, your brain snapped a picture of what your eyes saw, filed the picture away in the gray squishy stuff we call memory, and locked it in. And now, it's all there for the taking! It's yours! Use it! Work your brain; visualize what your eyes saw. Practice, practice, practice! And note, when you think you have it mastered, remember there is always more. What kind of steak was it? How old did the carnation appear to be? Was there a lemon in the tea? What color are the napkins? Get the picture? Dig deep. Work it, baby, work it. Think of your eyes and ears as barbells for the brain and do a few thousand mind presses.

As you progress with the game, kick your brain into high gear and make it earn its keep. Now, as you determine the items on the table at a glance, in infinite and precise detail, and can plot their location, set your brain to determining all of the things that need improvement on the table. This is the most important part of the game for you.

Question what you saw. Visualize the perfect table. On the perfect table, the salt would be full, and the salad forks (two of the four forks you saw) would have been removed some time ago. The carnation would have been fresh and in clean water. The iced tea would have plenty of ice, and the plate with a crumpled napkin in it would be gone, (obviously the diner is no longer interested in eating off a plate he has thrown a used napkin into). Once you begin to visualize the perfect table at a glance, and act on those visualizations, your tips, and your reputation, will begin to improve.

The perfect table is ever-changing. It has a perfect look for every moment it is in use — from a table ready for customers to be seated, to a table ready for the check. All points in between these two images also have their perfect look and moment. Think about it. Visualize it. A table where people are enjoying salads will look differently than that same table when the people are enjoying entrees. Visualizing the perfect table at every step of the way predisposes you to actually making it happen. Take it in at a glance; correct the problems in your brain; and then tell your hands to make it reality.

Your goal with the "I Spy" game, is to train your brain to act with the speed and thoroughness of the best spy on earth. Spontaneous attention to detail translates to big money. Your goal with your customers is to hear them say as you walk away, "Man, is our server *GREAT* !!" If you hear that, then you have won the game!

Eyes and ears. You've got some. Use them to **make more money**!

Chapter Five

Q & A

Questions and answers, and, . . . surprises?
And the Survey Says . . .

One of the best ways of looking at ourselves, is by looking through the eyes of others. I mentioned early, that as part of my research for this book, I asked people from across the nation to complete questionnaires about food service. I asked them to share their likes and dislikes, their pet peeves, and their kudos for great service. I also asked questions relating to what degree of importance they might place on a specific food server behavior. Some of the answers are obvious, but others may surprise you.

For this information to be of the most value to you, you must first complete the questionnaire yourself. By doing so, before you read the results of the majority, you will be providing yourself with an insightful gauge. Do you really know what people want from you? Are you in sync with what are the most important requirements in food service? Are you guilty of any of the negative behaviors described? Complete the questionnaire now, before reading any further. Remember, don't look at the survey answers before you complete the questionnaire yourself. In other words, don't cheat! (Never, ever lie to yourself!) The benefit of completing the questionnaire first, before reading on, is tremendous. Don't deny yourself the full impact of the information provided. I'm not attacking your integrity, but rather, trying to keep you from being just a little lazy and skipping this important exercise in awareness. So, get a pen, and do it now. . .

Food Service Questionnaire

Question 1:

On a scale of 1 to 10, with **1** being the **most important** and **10** being the **least important**, and by **using any number as often as you like** so that **each attribute** will have **its own score** (for example, you may end up with all 1's, all 10's, or, a variety of scores), please rate each **separate** attribute listed below according to the importance you place on a server exhibiting that quality:

____ Personal Cleanliness
(Hair, body, shoes, and uniform clean, no strong odors)

____ A Friendly Disposition
(Smiles, introduces themselves, seems to care)

____ A Good Memory
(Remembers to bring all necessary items required and who gets what)

____ Efficiency/Quick Response
(Doesn't dally, is quick to refill drinks, etc.)

____ Attentiveness
(Doesn't disappear during service, is around when you need them)

____ Awareness
(Predicts needs and resolves problems)

____ Knowledge of Menu and Restaurant
(Knows what's available and what isn't, what can or can't be done)

____ Ability To Do The Job
(Has the know-how and experience to be a server)

____ Helpfulness
(Makes suggestions, finds a way to accommodate you, etc.)

____ Other - please specify:_____

* * * * * * * *

Question 2:

To determine the most desirable traits in food service, you will score the same attributes once again. This time, using the **same attributes** that you just scored, **score them again**, only this time, use **each number**, 1 through 10, **only once**, rating the attributes against each other according to importance, (with **1** being **most important** and **10** being the **least important**). You will end up with only one "1", one "2", one "3", and so on through "10":

____ Personal Cleanliness
(Hair, body, shoes, and uniform clean, no strong odors)
____ A Friendly Disposition
(Smiles, introduces themselves, seems to care)
____ A Good Memory
(Remembers to bring all necessary items required and who gets what)
____ Efficiency/Quick Response
(Doesn't dally, is quick to refill drinks, etc.)
____ Attentiveness
(Doesn't disappear during service, is around when you need them)
____ Awareness
(Predicts needs and resolves problems)
____ Knowledge of Menu and Restaurant
(Knows what's available and what isn't, what can or can't be done)
____ Ability To Do The Job
(Has the know-how and experience to be a server)
____ Helpfulness
(Makes suggestions, finds a way to accommodate you, etc.)
____ Other - please specify:_____

****

Question 3:

Below are some very undesirable food server descriptions. Using the numbers 1 to 15 with **1** being the **worst offensive**, and **15** being the **least offensive**, and **using any number as often as you like** so that **each behavior** has **its own score** (for example, you may end up with all 15's, all 1's, or, a variety of scores), please rate each **separate** act according to what you hate to see most in food server behavior:

____ A server who is rude and argumentative
____ A server who talks excessively
____ A server who is wearing strong perfume, or smells of smoke or other disagreeable odors
____ A server who ignores you or disappears
____ A server who "gets the order wrong"
____ A server who moves like a snail
____ A server who is 'snobby' and acts as if waiting on you is an imposition
____ A server who is confused and clumsy
____ A server who serves dishes with food falling off or stuck to the outside
____ A server who looks dirty
____ A server who is too rushed to do a good job
____ A server who is too shy and timid
____ A server who is lazy
____ A server who can't remember anything
____ A server who: (please specify)_____

* * * * * * * *

Question 4:

To determine the most undesirable traits in food service, you will score the same bad behaviors once again. This time, using the **same behaviors** that you just scored, **score them again**, only this time, use **each number**, 1 through 15, **only once**, rating the behaviors against each other according to undesirability, (with **1** being **most offensive** and **15** being the **least offensive**). You will end up with only one "1", one "2", one "3", and so on through "15".

____ A server who is rude and argumentative
____ A server who talks excessively
____ A server who is wearing strong perfume, or smells of smoke or other disagreeable odors
____ A server who ignores you or disappears
____ A server who "gets the order wrong"
____ A server who moves like a snail
____ A server who is 'snobby' and acts as if waiting on you is an imposition
____ A server who is confused and clumsy
____ A server who serves dishes with food falling off or stuck to the outside
____ A server who looks dirty
____ A server who is too rushed to do a good job
____ A server who is too shy and timid
____ A server who is lazy
____ A server who can't remember anything
____ A server who: (please specify)_____

****

Question 5:
Please describe a personal **pet peeve** you have about food servers:

_____
_____
_____
_____
_____
_____

****

Question 6:
Please describe the **worst** food service **experience** you have ever had:

_____
_____
_____
_____
_____
_____

****

Question 7:
Please describe **something special** a food server did for you that you will never forget:

_____
_____
_____
_____
_____
_____

****

Question 8:

Please describe the **one thing** you care most about in food service:

_____
_____
_____
_____
_____
_____

****

Question 9:

Please make any other comments or observations that you think would make food service better:

_____
_____
_____
_____
_____
_____

****

Question 10:

What **percentage** of the check is your customary tip? _____%

****

Question 11:

Do you tip **more** (a bigger percentage) at fine dining establishments than you do at diners or chain restaurants?

Yes_____ No_____

****

Question 12:

Do you expect the servers to be better at fine dining establishments than at family restaurants or diners?

Yes_____ No_____

****

Question 13:

If you receive **exceptional** service, do you tip more than your customary percentage?

Yes_____ No_____

****

Question 14:

Name an example of what you consider to be exceptional service:
_____
_____
_____
_____
_____
_____

****

Question 15:

Name an example of server behavior that you consider to be **absolutely intolerable** and **unacceptable**:

_____
_____
_____
_____
_____
_____

****

Question 16:

Does it **bother** you to see your server. . .(please circle <u>Y</u>es or <u>N</u>o)

. . .talking with other servers when you need them?	Y	N
. . .sitting down while you are their customer?	Y	N
. . .smoking in view of customers?	Y	N
. . .eating in view of customers?	Y	N
. . .chatting about personal matters with other customers when you are trying to get their attention?	Y	N
. . .ignoring dirty dishes on your table?	Y	N
. . .running around frantically?	Y	N
. . .leaving in the middle of your service?	Y	N
. . .carrying too many plates and dishes at once?	Y	N
. . .moving like a snail?	Y	N
. . .being a pest by bothering you too much?	Y	N
. . .treating other customers differently than you?	Y	N

You are finished with the questionnaire.

HOORAY!!

Well, how do you think your answers will stack up against those of customers from all over the country? Don't be surprised if you have missed the boat from time to time. Psssst! I'll let you in on a little secret. I gave this questionnaire to some restaurant managers and owners themselves. Guess what; some of *them* didn't have a clue. That is very sad, indeed. However, you should know that the responses obtained from the restaurant managers and owners **were not included** in the results you are about to read. The primary purpose of the questionnaires was to ascertain **your customers'** feelings, not restaurant management feelings. That is why restaurant worker responses were excluded.

The responses provided by your customers give you an arsenal of information with which to improve your service. You now have the ability to respond to what your customers *really* want from you. If you can do that, you will **make more money**, and I've repeated it often enough, that's what this book is all about! **I want you to make more money!**

Remember our discussion about repetition? Well, you may have noticed while completing the questionnaire that I asked virtually the same question several times, only worded differently, in different sections. Why? I have found that for the real truth to emerge, one has to arrive at the same answer when the question has been asked in different manners. (If you think it isn't so, spend a little time in a courtroom, and watch an attorney work on a witness!) The importance of this kind of truth is tremendous. It is absolute. That is what has been accomplished here. You can take this information to the bank. You don't need to think about it and rationalize to yourself that perhaps something is not 'really all that important' because the room for error on these important issues has been virtually eliminated. When you read the following answers, you had better accept them, because they are the laws you need to work by. The people who have been gracious enough to share of their personal time to complete these questionnaires have given you a great gift. If you choose not to accept that gift, you lose. Let's look at the responses.

In addition to the questions asked in the survey, I also obtained background information on the persons who completed the questionnaires. You will be interested to know that the answers came from restaurant diners across the country. Note the following about the respondents who completed the questionnaire:

— 69% were female — 31% were male

— of the females, 67% were under the age of 50 — 33% were over the age of 50

— of the males, 50% were under the age of 50 — 50% were over the age of 50

— collectively, 62% of all respondents were under the age of 50 — 38% were over the age of 50

— of the females, 83% were non-smokers — 17% were smokers

— of the males, 56% were non-smokers — 31% were smokers — and 13% failed to provide their smoking status.

— Collectively, 75% of all people who completed the questionnaire were non-smokers — 21% were smokers — and 4% did not specify.

(The smoking statistics reflect a parallel to the national smoking statistics which confirm that the vast majority of people in our society are non-smokers.)

And the survey says!. . .

Question 1:

(Remember, "1" is **most important**, and "10" is **least important** to our respondents — *your* customers)

	Score:	**%:**
Personal Cleanliness:	1	82%
	2	16%
	3	2%
		100%

(Interesting note: all of the 2% who rated Personal Cleanliness as only a "3" in their book, were smokers, which supports my earlier assertion that non-smokers are *more demanding* than smokers — *"more demanding"*, as applied here, means being held to a *higher standard of conduct*)

A Friendly Disposition:	1	61%
	2	9%
	3	20%
	4	5%
	5	5%
		100%

A Good Memory:	1	52%
	2	16%
	3	18%
	4	7%
	5	5%
	6	0%
	7	2%
		100%

Efficiency/Quick Response:	1	41%
	2	32%
	3	18%
	4	7%
	5	<u>2%</u>
		100%
Attentiveness:	1	42%
	2	36%
	3	18%
	4	2%
	5	<u>2%</u>
		100%
Awareness:	1	30%
	2	32%
	3	23%
	4	7%
	5	5%
	6	1%
	7	1%
	8	<u>1%</u>
		100%
Knowledge:	1	47%
	2	11%
	3	20%
	4	9%
	5	7%
	6	2%
	7	0%
	8	2%
	9	<u>2%</u>
		100%

Ability To Do The Job:	1	57%
	2	11%
	3	20%
	4	5%
	5	<u>7%</u>
		100%

Helpfulness:	1	27%
	2	32%
	3	25%
	4	9%
	5	<u>7%</u>
		100%

Well, how do your answers compare to those of your customers? Are you surprised by any of them? Did the importance you attach to each of these attributes match the importance clearly specified by your dining public? Before we discuss more, let's look at the answer to Question 2.

Question 2:

(Remember that each number is only used once here, with "1" being the most important. This list is *prioritized*.)

Score		Attribute
1	=	Personal Cleanliness
2	=	A Friendly Disposition
3	=	Ability To Do The Job
4	=	A Good Memory
5	=	Knowledge of Menu And Restaurant
6	=	Attentiveness
7	=	Efficiency/Quick Response
8	=	Awareness
9	=	Helpfulness

Were you "on the money" with your priorities? Are you surprised to learn that "Personal Cleanliness" (your appearance and odor) is the **number one** food server quality desired most by restaurant customers across the country? Were you aware that "Personal Cleanliness" and "Friendly Disposition" outrank the "Ability To Do The Job"? Are you amazed to learn that "A Good Memory" is so far above "Efficiency/Quick Response"? This information should open your eyes to what your customers truly want from you. Pay attention, and your tips will grow.

Having just one of the qualities is not enough; you must have them all — in abundance! Remember, all of these attributes together are what truly makes the exceptional server, the one who makes the most money.

You will recall that **Questions 1** and **2** contained a place for "Other". What do you think was written in here most often on the questionnaires? Stumped? The most frequently written-in response in this area was: "A Good Listener". The customers wrote of their frustrations in having servers repeatedly get the orders wrong because they did not truly listen to the orders as they were given. As a write-in, it would place 10th in the list of priorities. However, I must ask this question: Would it have ranked so low if I had included it myself in the list of attributes when I created the questionnaire? If I had, everyone who completed a survey would have seen it. Under that circumstance, I do not think it would have been last. I think it would have actually placed very high. I didn't think to put it there, (alas, we're all quite fallible) but the responding public let me know that it is so very important. This proves even more emphatically that servers must learn from as many sources as possible and not limit their training or growing to their immediate environment or to only one research or practice. Listening to your customers, whether taking their order, or just overhearing their comments or frustrations, is one of the most valuable ways to do this. "A Good Listener" is a very important quality in anyone, especially in a food server.

Give the information learned here your immediate attention. Don't disregard the lower scores, like "Helpfulness", which came in at number "9" in the prioritized response to **Question 2**. In **Question**

2, customers were *forced* to prioritize, and something *had* to be at the bottom. But remember, according to the responses to **Question 1**, "Helpfulness" was given a number "1" score by 27% of the people, number "2" by 32% of the people, and number "3" by 25% of the people. That means that even though "Helpfulness" was scored in the prioritized list at number "9", that, in truth, a whopping 84% of your customers consider it to be of paramount importance to them. The moral here is simple. I've said it before. If you can please the most demanding customer, then all of the others will be a cake walk. The answers you see here tell you how extremely important all of these attributes truly are.

Question 3:

(Remember, of the behaviors listed, "1" is the **worst offensive** and "15" is the **least offensive** to our respondents — *your* customers)

These are scores for servers who. . .

are rude or argumentative:

	Score:	%
	1	80%
	2	5%
	3	10%
	4	5%
		100%

talk excessively:

	1	26%
	2	10%
	3	21%
	4	5%
	5	3%
	6	5%
	7	5%
	8	3%
	9	0%
	10	10%
	11	3%
	12	0%
	13	5%
	14	0%
	15	<u>4%</u>
		100%

smells of smoke or strong perfume or other strong odors:

	1	62%
	2	13%
	3	10%
	4	4%
	5	3%
	6	<u>8%</u>
	100%	

ignores you or disappears:

	1	69%
	2	10%
	3	10%
	4	3%
	5	<u>8%</u>
		100%

gets the order wrong:

1	38%
2	10%
3	23%
4	8%
5	3%
6	5%
7	3%
8	5%
9	0%
10	3%
11	0%
12	2%
	100%

moves like a snail:

1	33%
2	23%
3	10%
4	13%
5	5%
6	4%
7	3%
8	3%
9	3%
10	2%
11	0%
12	1%
	100%

is snobby and acts as if waiting on customer is an imposition:

1	72%
2	15%
3	0%
4	3%
5	3%
6	3%
7	0%
8	0%
9	0%
10	3%
11	0%
12	1%
	100%

are confused and clumsy:

1	26%
2	15%
3	13%
4	13%
5	10%
6	3%
7	3%
8	8%
9	3%
10	3%
11	-
	100%

serve dishes with food falling off or stuck to them:

	1	44%
	2	15%
	3	13%
	4	5%
	5	13%
	6	3%
	7	0%
	8	0%
	9	0%
	10	3%
	11	0%
	12	3%
	13	<u>1%</u>
		100%

looks dirty:

	1	87%
	2	8%
	3	<u>5%</u>
		100%

is too rushed to do a good job:

	1	21%
	2	26%
	3	10%
	4	8%
	5	15%
	6	15%
	7	0%
	8	0%
	9	0%
	10	<u>5%</u>
		100%

is too shy and timid:

	1	10%
	2	10%
	3	5%
	4	8%
	5	21%
	6	13%
	7	5%
	8	5%
	9	0%
	10	10%
	11	0%
	12	0%
	13	0%
	14	3%
	15	<u>10%</u>
		100%

is lazy:

	1	38%
	2	28%
	3	8%
	4	5%
	5	8%
	6	5%
	7	0%
	8	5%
	9	0%
	10	<u>3%</u>
		100%

can't remember anything:

	1	44%
	2	31%
	3	5%
	4	3%
	5	3%
	6	5%
	7	4%
	8	3%
	9	2%
		100%

Do the preceding figures ring any bells? Can you honestly look at your own service and say you are not guilty of any of these extremely undesirable behaviors?

To put these figures in perspective, let's concentrate on the **top three numbers** in each category. We can agree that out of a possible spread of 1 to 15, that those customers marking numbers **1, 2, or 3**, are **very serious** about their dislike of any behavior they marked that way. By **combining the scores of the top three positions**, for **each** separate behavior, a very clear message emerges. This is how it looks:

100% of the customers (that's **everybody**, folks) marked "a server who looks dirty" as absolutely offensive and intolerable server behavior. This more than confirms the responses given in **Questions 1** and **2** wherein "Personal Cleanliness" emerged as the most important quality in a food server. You can clearly see that even though the questions were asked differently the answer is the same. (Review Piglets and Roaches)

95% of the customers marked "a server who is rude and argumentative" as clearly repulsive server behavior. (Review Bulls)

95% of the customers marked "a server who is snobby and acts as if waiting on you is an imposition" as undeniably awful behavior. (Review Cats)

89% of the customers cited "a server who ignores you or disappears" as unacceptable behavior. (Review Ostriches)

85% of the customers expressed complete dismay and offense at "a server who is wearing strong perfume, or smells of smoke or other disagreeable odors". (Review Skunks)

80% of the customers named "a server who can't remember anything" as disagreeable server behavior. (Review Dodo Birds)

74% of the customers were extremely turned off by "a server who is lazy". (Review Sloths)

72% of the customers declared their revulsion of "a server who serves dishes with food falling off or stuck to the outside". (Review Pack Mules)

71% of the customers were not accepting of "a server who gets the order wrong". (Review Dodo Birds and Mice)

66% of the customers found "a server who moves like a snail" to be very bad server behavior. (Review Snails)

57% of the customers were offended by "a server who talks excessively". (Review Parrots)

57% of the customers would not accept "a server who is too rushed to do the job", [although one extremely astute respondent made a notation on their questionnaire that this may be a 'management problem'. In many cases, that is very true, and very sad; but it is not always management's fault!] (Review Roadrunners)

54% of the customers don't tolerate "a server who is confused and clumsy". (Review Dodo Birds)

These are staggering numbers! The only area where your customers are inclined to give anyone a break, are the servers who "are too shy and timid", (Review Mice), where only **25%** of the responding customers cited this behavior as extremely offensive. **But, that is just the point. 25%** are *very turned off* by this behavior. Now, try to imagine if this is your only bad behavior just how much that translates to in lost tips. **25% — a full one fourth —** of your customers will react negatively to this behavior!

You must work hard to eliminate **ALL** of these bad behaviors. Some of them will impact your tips more than others, but guaranteed, anytime you act in a way that offends your customer, you are delivering a death blow to your tips! So imagine, just for a moment, that you have approached the table in a stained uniform, smelling of strong perfume, holding a messy plate, and forgetting 'who got what' when you got there. Shiver me timbers! It's not a pretty picture. You have positively hurt yourself. Why would you even bother to go to work if you are not prepared to be the best and make the most?!

Question 3:

Question 3 also had a place for "Other", allowing the respondents to fill in additional distressing bad behaviors that were important to them. Some of the most interesting were: a server who. . .

"flirts with my husband" (Shame on you hussies out there who did this, tsk, tsk.)

"spends your mealtime telling you their life's history and miseries" (Told you so - don't do this - ever)

"forgets to give me the check and I have to ask them for it" (A job is never completed until the paperwork is done!)

"chews gum" (Tell me you never do this, yuk!)

"counts their tips in view of me then comments to co-workers in reference to the amount" (Heavens people, tips are private!)

"uses foul language" (You've got to be kidding! If I ever heard this, I would not rest until that server was bounced like a rubber ball — *unbelievable!*)

"combs hair in view of customers" (*Hello. . .* ? Who would do such a thing!)

"is more interested in the tip than giving service" (Remember Slug-A-Bed?)

"leaves food sitting on counter under heat lamps; you can see it and it is not served immediately" (I told you they notice these things!)

"doesn't speak English well" (Well, duh. Communication is vital; this is an English-speaking country; if you need to: practice, practice, practice!)

"is not apologetic upon errors" (This is a bad habit so very many servers are guilty of — a few people skills go a long, long way, my friends)

"waits on me with a cold" ("Cold in the head - build a fire in the belly" is my personal safeguard against the common cold. Lots of Vitamin C, raw onions, garlic, and Tabasco works for me. As you aggressively seek *your* cure of choice, whether it's vitamins or spicy foods or chicken soup or howling at the moon, just remember to be considerate and quit hacking on your customers. And for heaven's sake, wash your hands again and again. If you are sick or contagious, don't work — just think of the number of people you can contaminate!)

"gives me silverware off another table" (There's that nasty old Sloth again!)

"bugs the hell out of me" (Ah, there's the clue — service must be attentive without being intrusive, and it surely can be that way — serve; don't bother)

"tastes the food in front of me" (NO WAY!! I assume what this customer is referring to is observing a server popping a tidbit into their mouth in the bus station or perhaps in the kitchen [where, unfortunately, they can still be seen], and not truly sampling someone's fare. In any event, anytime you are in front of your customers, your *hands* should be involved in this job, not your smacking lips!)

"doesn't listen" (There it is again. Your customers want to be *heard* and *understood*, and that requires someone who truly does listen!)

There were many other write-ins which were variations of the same issues we have already discussed. There were also a few that even I don't have the nerve to put into print. (And I have never been accused of having no nerve!) Suffice it to say, your customers are acutely aware of your every behavior. If you want to make a great deal of money in tips, there's no question that you absolutely, positively, must eliminate these bad, repulsive, annoying, distressing, shameful behaviors. For every little one you keep, even only in part, you are bludgeoning your tips. It makes no sense to put in all those tiring hours and then take home the equivalent of an eight-year-old's allowance. It doesn't have to be that way. You can make big money if you apply the effort! It's fundamentally true that you are what you eat. It's also true that you reap what you sow. Accept it. Build from it.

Succeed beyond your wildest dreams. Success is built into all of us; it's just that some of us beat it to death because failure serves us better. Before I wax too philosophical, let me just say that if you accept anything, accept that you are 100% responsible for your own actions. You are 100% responsible for the amount of money you make as a food server. You are 100% responsible for your success — or failure.

Question 4:

(Remember that each number is only used once here, and number "1" is the *most hated* bad behavior)

A server who:

Score	Bad Behavior
1	looks dirty
2	is rude and argumentative
3	is snobby
4	ignores you or disappears
5	smells of strong perfume or smoke, etc.
6	serves dishes with food falling off or stuck to them
7	can't remember anything
8	is lazy
9	gets the order wrong
10	moves like a snail
11	talks excessively
12	is confused and clumsy
13	is too rushed to do a good job
14	is too shy and timid

How did your list stack up to this one? Did you pinpoint the seriousness of the various problems? Were your views of bad habits of the same priority as your customers? Listen to your customers. This list is a beacon. It's a bright, flashing neon sign. It's the hammer that is hitting you on the head. **Pay attention!** Clean up your act if you need to; and reap the benefits of this information. You will never again have the excuse, "I didn't know". Your customers are shouting their feelings at you!

Question 5:

In this question, I asked the respondents to describe a **personal pet peeve**. Some of them are doozies; here are my favorites:

"food servers who aren't friendly, enjoyable, and attentive" (Well, that about covers it don't you think?)
"a server who snaps at me" (There's that rude old Bull again)
"a server who is unfamiliar with the menu" (This really is annoying; we've discussed it before, but it deserves mentioning again)
"ignorance of serving techniques and the serving establishment" (Basically a reiteration of the above statement, only more emphatic — see how important it is?)
"food served cold or just warm" (People hate this! I hate this! All servers should hate this! It's unthinkable! The customer who wrote this went on to offer a suggestion that food be covered when it comes to the table. This is not always possible. Many restaurants are simply not equipped for such luxury. Getting the food from the docks to the table in a flash is the real answer. Note: nearly 50% of the pet peeves written in dealt with this subject!)
"acts rude to children" (This topic could have had its own chapter, but I decided against it. I will, instead, briefly address the issue here. Okay, I sympathize; kids can be a burden to a food server. Many *parents* act pathetically in a restaurant and fail to guide and control their children. But, the truth is, kids are people too. Further, they are the apple of their parents' eyes. Mess with their kids and you have ventured beyond the point of no return. You might as well kiss your tip good-bye. After all, it's the parents who do the tipping. It's often helpful to remember that children's behavior is a direct result of parenting. The children themselves, especially very young children, most likely bear a great deal less fault in their actions than their parents bear. It's usually the parents who need the good spanking. Think of that when you serve children. Act accordingly, and be nice to them. Give them the benefit of the doubt because many children are the most delightful human beings you will ever meet.)

"when they rush you inappropriately — I remember one time I had waited a while for my meal; after about only five minutes, the server asked if I was through and was going to take my plate and I had barely started eating" (Unfortunately, this is a common enough occurrence. What drives a server to act this way? Stop it!)

"a long waiting period between being seated and having meal served; i.e.: takes a while to have order taken and a long while for meal to be served; like if appetizers are complimentary, they should be served immediately, not after you have other food" (Well, I'm stunned; apparently Sloths and Snails are multiplying like rabbits out there. It's a deplorable state of affairs that this type of bad service is so widely exhibited across this country. Get over it! Your dining public is putting its foot down. We don't have to accept and pay for bad service; and we aren't going to!)

"some have a tendency to not pay enough attention to individual patrons and try to wait on too many people; individual attention to each customer is important" (You heard it here; people want to be served attentively and properly and not be made to feel like cattle on an assembly line.)

"when they accidentally stick their thumb in the food and then stick their thumb in their mouth — and I have seen that more than a time or two — you know that sound it makes when you suck food off of your thumb? ewe!" (This one cracks me up, but I think this customer said it plain enough!!` Yuk-a-roony!)

"a server who chews and pops her gum" (The fact that this appeared so incredibly often is shocking to me. What the heck's going on out there? Try a breath mint for pete's sake, but quit chomping. Your customers are extremely offended! Good grief.)

"the job is beneath them, so they think or appear" (Attention Cats and Roaches! I've said this 'til I'm blue in the face — love it or leave it — simple.)

"doesn't refill drinks without being asked" (I just don't get it. When you are a customer, don't you want your drinks full? Don't you want to be attended to? Think like a customer; care about your customers; anticipate their needs and desires.)

"servers who take your order and disappear for long periods of time with no service or explanations" (Ostriches, take heed!)

"all waiters or waitresses should be able to understand English when working in an American place, or at least have someone who does" (This pet peeve was repeated so many times, I must accept that managers out there are not in tune with their buying public at all. As a server, you have a responsibility to make yourself be understood. If you don't speak fluent English, take a course; practice with a tape recorder; get tutored; do whatever it takes. Your lack of a strong command of the English language will affect your tips — whether you believe it is right for that to happen or not. I believe in a world order. I believe none of us are more important than others. But I also believe, as obviously your customers believe, that "when in Rome" as the saying goes, "do as the Romans". You are in an English-speaking country; speak English. If any of your customers travel to your native home, you can demand they speak your native language. Fair is fair.)

"bad attitude - I was a waitress for years and cannot abide rude behavior, sloppy service - I know one can give good service and pride in appearance" (You heard it from a customer who was once one of your own!)

"long hair not tied back or otherwise protected from falling in food" (All right all you lady and lad Godivas, no one likes hairy food. It really turns the old guts so, please, tame that mane! I'm not advocating hair nets, can't abide them myself, [except for cooks, who really *do* need them], but there are other ways, use them!)

"one who when pouring coffee slops it all over; also, one who gets upset when you say your food is cold, and doesn't offer to take it back" (Well, this respondent covered a couple of points that involve a nice combination of Sloth, Bull, Cat, Dodo Bird and Roach behaviors. See how easy it is to get caught in those behaviors? Your customers notice; don't think they don't.)

"not taking care of needs when asked; slow in granting request for something" (Sloth, Cat, Snail, Bull, Sloth, Cat, Snail, Bull,

Sloth, Cat, Snail, Bull - shame, shame, shame)

- **"cup of coffee half full, served in a cold cup; servers who serve regular coffee when you specified decafe, and your system has trouble tolerating caffeine"** (Folks, this is serious, indeed. The first part of this pet peeve is a common annoyance, a typical Slothful behavior. The second part is dangerous. It pointedly affects your customers' health. Any time a customer is specific about a food or food additive, you must absolutely, without fail, honor their instructions. Eggs instead of "egg beaters" can damage persons under doctor's care. Regular coffee instead of decafe can cause undue suffering or worse. Butter instead of margarine can cause a dairy-intolerant person to have an adverse reaction. You must listen and respond appropriately. Many people have allergic reactions to certain foods or additives. Some nuts are that way for me. If I ask whether or not a certain food has nuts and I am told "no", but it turns out that it does have nuts [even crushed into oblivion], it is more than likely I will be sick. Rosemary will trigger an asthma attack for me. If you don't know, ask the cooks. Don't guess. Don't play with people's lives. You may think people are being just "too fussy". Not so. When your customers ask you about a specific food or spice or additive, or specify decafe over regular, or margarine over butter, etc., it is imperative you honor those wishes to the letter. **To the letter!** This issue has a greater importance than just your tips — a *much* greater importance. Don't fail in this; it could literally cost someone their health, or even their life.)
- **"persons who interfere with patrons conversations no matter what the conversation is about"** (Parrots, are you listening? Restrain yourself.)
- **"I can't stand seeing someone who is seated after me get waited on before me"** (An obvious no-no, and believe me, your customers don't give a flying fig if those people seated after them are in someone else's station. It just doesn't matter. Get to new customers quickly and don't subject them to watching latecomers get served first or you can kiss off a potential great tip.)

"a server who lets you know how busy they are to the point that they cannot handle the job - makes me wonder why I am sitting in that station, etc." (There is nothing wrong with a comment like "I have an order that just came up, I'll be with you in just a moment". Such a comment says that you are busy, but that you care about your other customers. But to say something like, "I'm just so busy" or "I'm really busy" is just not acceptable. The inference of those types of statements is that, *"Hey, I'm already overloaded, what the heck do you want of me!"* Big difference. If you eliminate all of the bad behaviors, and organize properly, there will be plenty of time to adequately serve *all* of your customers effectively. There will never be a need to declare your "busyness". Remember, customers do not want to feel like an imposition.)

"I hate servers who make comments about the way I eat, like 'you didn't eat your vegetables' or 'boy, did you clean your plate!'" (Hey, you're not their mother! Keep it to yourself!)

"being seated in a non-smoking area that is right next to smoking; nobody ever tells the smoke it's supposed to stay in the smoking section" (This is pretty funny, but true. Humans are notoriously slow at picking up on the obvious, aren't we? We can't train smoke; we can only make sure there isn't any.)

"I dislike food servers who complain - about their shift, hours, wages, other customers, or the cooks or busboys - these are also the types who like to tell you about their ex-spouses, dying children, or sick pets - it's incredible the things they think you want to know about them" (Complainers, be gone! This customer said it so well.)

"hating their job" (Why should customers reward you for hating your job?)

"when they talk themselves up all the time hoping to get a big tip; or try to play on your sympathy to get a big tip" (They're on to you; give it up; it only makes you look foolish - exceptional service is what creates big tips, not bragging or sob stories.)

"many times I don't get what I ordered in restaurants and fast food places, so I hate people who don't listen" (There's that listening again. Let me just ask you something. Do you think people don't notice when they have the wrong food? You can't possibly believe that do you? Then why did this pet peeve keep cropping up? There must be a reason. You're not listening out there! Open those ears and engage that brain!)

"being rushed or ignored - they're both terrible to me" (I agree. They are both equally terrible.)

"putting your check down in a puddle" (What is that puddle doing there in the first place? Tables should be clean; checks should be clean. You bet this is annoying.)

"a server who lights a cigarette, takes a couple of drags, then puts it out and goes right on with their job" (Holy cow, I am beyond disgusted; how gross can one get! This isn't a pet peeve, it's a crime!)

Question 6:

In **Question 6**, I asked the respondents to describe the worst food experience they have ever had. Here's a sampling:

"food didn't arrive until an hour after order - some items cold, some burnt" (There is no excuse whatsoever for this type of action; it should have been beneath the server's own dignity to serve a meal this way!)

"30 minutes before order was taken, another 15 minutes before meal was served" (Same song, same sad state of affairs.)

"waiter spilled wine all over my companion, he got the order wrong — total nightmare" (Let me share with you the fact that this customer was so incensed, that in addition to the above statement, they also included the name and location of the establishment in their write-in. What does that tell you? If they remembered this horrible experience so clearly as to include specific details in a survey years later, how many times do you think they have repeated it to other people? My guess would be oodles. This server not only did himself in by his improper behavior, he killed the chances for that restaurant to ever get this customer back. Further, the bad reputation of both server, and establishment, spreads like wildfire.

Reread the Bull server section and never be guilty of destroying customers for yourself or your restaurant.)

"patron ignored; wrong food delivered" (It bears repeating, customers hate server inadequacies!)

"the waitress was very unfriendly; when we needed her, she was never around" (This customer, too, specified the restaurant and location. Your customers are like elephants; they never forget! Let them remember good things, not distressing things like this!)

"very long wait for service and meal; basically ignored" (There's a definite pattern here, folks)

"several have been rude and ignored me as a customer; forgetting food after it has been prepared and letting it get cold" (Obviously, this customer has seen this behavior repeated often. Yet, I would bet my bottom dollar that these servers blamed *the customers* for "being bad tippers")

"ordered toast and milk with breakfast; received toast and milk ten minutes after I was served breakfast" (Organization, Organization, Organization!)

"I was served raw chicken, sent it back, it was still raw; never made it right and never offered compensation" (People really are entitled to **cooked** food. Oh, duh. If the cooks do this to you, apprise the manager of it immediately! The cooks need cooking lessons; the customer needs compensating; and you need to bend over backwards to rectify the problem any way you can. This is totally, unequivocally unacceptable!)

"witnessing a server emerging from a filthy restroom and then commencing to handle food" (This server may have washed their hands thoroughly, but it didn't matter because the restroom itself was dirty. A filthy restroom is a management problem. If your restaurant is not clean, look for a new job!)

"ignored for ten minutes after being seated; order in process for too long; order wrong in 2 or 3 material aspects" (Sloth, Dodo Bird, Cat, Bull - get with the program. Can't you see how this sticks in people's craws? Can't you see why these people would not be inclined to tip you? No excuse.)

"**watching a waiter eat from a dish he was about to serve**" (What a turnoff! Unbelievable how this keeps popping up — major disgusting — worth a big fat zero tip — worth being fired over.)

"**a cockroach served in the food**" (Nothing more need be said.)

"**ordered a regular dinner menu item; there was an appetizer item of the same thing on menu; when food came, was served the appetizer size; called our waiter and he said it was correct; so did 2 other waiters we asked; finally had to call manager who said it was the wrong size item and got us the right one**" (Stubborn Bulls! How much time do you suppose elapsed during all of this questioning? What was happening to all of the other served food? What were the other patrons at the table doing during this fiasco? How incredibly poor service this was. This server should be ashamed. If he were a crew member on a ship, I'd suggest having him keelhauled! And for two other servers to actually corroborate the error, tells me that this was one incredibly poorly-trained group of servers. The manager failed miserably in his management of these servers, but fortunately, handled the customer properly. Managers must realize that any error by any worker under them, is their own personal error and act accordingly. This manager did so. I can only hope that after making all things right with this customer, the manager did not fail in his duty to the servers — by letting their error slide with no further discussion. These servers *definitely* need enlightenment. This incident so affected this customer that they consider it their worst-ever dining experience. The Bull server not only failed to know his own menu and restaurant, he basically called the customer a liar. Pathetic.)

"**waitress was in restroom smoking pot and came out reeking of it; she was dismissed by the manager**" (Well, at least this had the appropriate conclusion; although I personally may have included the police in her 'dismissal'. Bringing drugs to work is so beyond rational thought. *Using* drugs is beyond rational thought!)

"**in a small restaurant, had ordered soup; when she brought it she set it down at the end of the table and shoved it across, spilling it all over; she was mad, she said, because she was too busy**"

(How is a customer supposed to react to this? I don't get it. How could this server expect any type of compensation for her service? Your state of pressure is of no concern to your customers. They expect, and have a right to expect, good service. If there is an available table for them in a restaurant, and they have been seated, then they should be served attentively and properly. This Sloth/Dodo Bird/Roadrunner/Bull server needs serious organizational training as well as serious 'people skills' training. Granted, there will always be moments, from time to time, where, by a twist of fate, you are faced with doing a zillion things at once. But the truth is, you can virtually eliminate that possibility with appropriate organization and personal control of your work day. Behaving as this server did is a lose-lose situation for all.)

"**the waitress served me pancakes that were white**" (Well, I'm not sure I have a clue what this customer is talking about. Perhaps it was snowing in the kitchen? Perhaps the pancake batter was old? Undercooked? I don't know. The point here is that the customer blamed the server. They clearly felt the server should have known better than to serve white pancakes. The moral of the story is know your menu. It's probably a pretty safe bet that pancakes are not supposed to be white. A server is ultimately responsible for anything put before a customer. If a cook gives you something that is obviously wrong, bad, or has items missing, it is *your responsibility* to see to it that it is corrected *before* the customer sees it.)

"**(1) eating in a restaurant with a bug catcher above the table; when requested that we be placed at another table; waitress appeared rude and annoyed; (2) watching the waiter drink beer as he throws his knives in the air for customers; (3) waitress who opened package with her teeth**" (Frankly, I'm not so sure I would eat in a restaurant that felt the need to annihilate bugs over my table. But if I did, you can bet I wouldn't want to be sitting directly under such a contraption. The server should have relocated this customer with a smile and then relayed the reason to her manager. One would hope that after a few such instances, the manager would get the hint and remove the bug blaster, or, the table under it. Some answers are just so dang obvious, aren't they?

As to experience number two, unless this routine is part of an established floor show, I would advise this server to consider a career switch to the circus. As for the beer drinking while on the job, I can't think of a single excuse for such behavior, ever. This server obviously thought he was amusing one table of customers, and thereby increasing his own tips, but he was actually making other customers nervous and upset. I don't know what more to say. This behavior is so bizarre; I can't find any justification whatsoever.

Item number three is more common. I have seen it happen frequently myself, especially with coffee grounds packets, etc. Use a pair of scissors. Your customers can't abide the thought of your saliva slithering, soggy and silent, onto whatever is inside the package you are opening. Save your teeth for opening things at home, or for presenting a big bright smile.)

"we were seated fast; silverware and water brought but no menu; finally got menu but no server took our order; finally ordered; appetizers came in fifteen minutes; salad came in another fifteen minutes; dinner got there and order was wrong; no apologies and the really bad part was we had our kids with us, ages 4 and 6, and they were cranky from all of the delay" (This type of generally bad service is truly repulsive to me. There are no valid excuses for affecting people's lives this way. There are no valid excuses for not having the common sense and decency to apologize for such failing behavior. These types of servers are death blows to a restaurant and to all of the other servers who work there. Don't behave this way; and don't tolerate it in others. This customer named names — from the name of the establishment to the name of the server. See how it sticks?!)

"birthday dinner, 1992; ran out of type of food we had ordered and couldn't make any substitutions of any relevance, and didn't tell us until it was too late to go somewhere else; they didn't tell us until after the soup and salad" (My heart breaks when I hear of something like this. Not only did the restaurant fail the customer, the server compounded the problem by not being on top of things. These behaviors not only destroyed a meal;

they ruined a birthday celebration. Chefs know if something is going to run out, long before it actually does. If they don't, they are performing their own jobs poorly. This was primarily a management problem. It was made worse by the server's lack of responsibility to their customer and their failure to go out of their way to make things right. The respondent also wrote of her date's extreme distress: **"because of his feelings for me, and wanting for my birthday to be special, he became obnoxious to the management staff over all the problems, and the whole night was ruined for me"**. This date's reaction was extreme. The whole situation escalated into something that was not salvageable for anyone involved. Everyone lost. Needless to say, I'm sure these people never returned to that restaurant. I would also bet they badmouthed the restaurant every time a birthday was mentioned. When will we understand that we are totally 100% responsible for our actions? And because of that responsibility, we will always be required to face the consequences of those actions. The only thing worse than a bad server is a bad manager. The combination of the two is insane. If you cause someone distress, it is your obligation to correct the problem while offering a sincere apology. Then treat them to something above and beyond an apology, something that overshadows the bad experience with a good one. Little things go a very long way.)

"**I think the cook waited on us; she was not well-groomed, and was slow; food was not hot; she served our plates to another table, and then, after a few minutes, simply moved the plates to our table where they belonged; all we had was salad and a pasta dish but were there over two hours, and had to remind her we needed our check; she told us to pay at the register, where she served as cashier, also!; the food had good flavor and tasted good, but we'll never go there again because of the service**" (Owners, listen up: GOOD FOOD ALONE DOES NOT A RESTAURANT MAKE!!!!)

"**the server dropped my food; looked to see if I was looking; I guess he thought I wasn't because he picked up, put it on the plate and served it to me! I couldn't help myself; I threw it at**

him" (Drastic, but effective. I do not advocate violence, in anything; but if you do such a thing, you deserve to be covered in food — at the very least.)
- **"when you order meat cooked medium and it is burned on the outside and raw on the inside"** (Cook's problem. However, remember that it is ultimately *your* responsibility to serve the food as it was ordered by the customer. It is also your responsibility to immediately correct any problem the chef has created for you. The chef's failures become your failures, just as your failures become management's failures.)
- **"once, a large group of us went to eat; we had gone in a day in advance to make sure they could accommodate us and we were told 'no problem'; when we arrived the following day, no one knew about us and the restaurant was short-staffed; needless to say the service was awful, and, the staff acted like we were interrupting their evening"** (Lack of communication between staff members destroys efficiency and destroys reputations. I find it hard to understand why any server would not get down on their knees and beg for large parties. They are no harder to serve than small parties if you are properly organized. As a bonus, the opportunity for a substantial tip is surefire. 'Short-staffed' is just an excuse. It just doesn't matter. If you can't accommodate the customers, don't seat them in the first place. If you don't have a system for noting large parties coming in, get out of the business. No excuses.)
- **"dirty dishes, waiter dirty; we left"** (I don't blame them. Piglets need not apply.)
- **"on a flight to Hawaii, service was the worst and we didn't see anyone on the plane eat the food"** (If you serve food, whether it is in a restaurant, a food booth, a plane, a train, a boat, or wherever, you are under the same scrutiny by your customers. Flight attendants are not exempt from the responsibility of good service just because their customers are captive and can't get up and walk out. [Walking out of a flying airplane can be extremely bad for your health.] This customer named the airlines in their response and I'm sure it has affected the airline's reputation

many times over. No business can survive repeated bad word of mouth. None.)

"driving through a fast food place and getting home and discovering that part of my order is missing" (We have all experienced this. It's a rampant problem. Again, while this does not relate to a typical sit-down restaurant, it is so important to realize that if you are a food server, of any type, you are still responsible to your customers. Fast food servers generally do not receive tips, but that is not an excuse for continual errors. Many fast food servers do eventually become servers in sit-down restaurants. Bad habits learned in fast food establishments are carried with them. Fast food servers are less likely to understand the concept of "reaping what you sow", and their transition to a table server is difficult. It doesn't have to be that way if they learn good service from the start — whether fast food, or not. Fast food servers are often teenagers working their first job. Training is never more important than it is during your first experience in the workplace. My very first job, at the age of fourteen, was as a waitress in a rustic lodge. I am ever grateful for that experience. For me it was a good one. Having a good first work experience sets a tone. Managers, please listen.)

"closing early after taking my order; standing by door; waiting for me to eat my food" (How awful. Not only did this restaurant not deserve this customer's repeat business, they did not deserve his business in the first place.)

"paying no attention to us and talking to others as serving" (I'd say this was a typical Cat/Parrot server who really doesn't have clue. Tips are based on performance. Don't ever forget it!)

"we were seated and given water, but no waitress came by; we were ignored completely even though they weren't busy; we had to leave" (I can't imagine having a business where the customer means so little. I can't imagine being a server who shows up for work, puts in the hours, and then complains that "I don't make any money at this job". I can't imagine wasting my life in this manner.)

There were so very many more horrible experiences, but a great number of them were related to topics we have already visited. A large percentage of them named names, dates, and places, proving just how much a bad experience sticks in our minds. The dining public is fed up with bad service, and rightfully so. If you want to make great tips, you must listen to the horror stories and learn from them. You must listen to the priorities of your customers, and do a serious self-examination of your own work habits. Get organized, and be the best you can be.

Question 7:

On the flip side, customers also have very strong memories of the *special* treatment they received while dining. In **Question 7**, I asked the respondents to describe something special that a food server did for them which they will never forget. Here is a sampling of some very positive (and some quite unusual) responses:

"we found something that didn't belong in a salad, and without being asked, the server took it back and took it off the price of the bill" (I don't know what was in there, and a vivid imagination could conjure up just about a million things that might not belong in a salad — from a French fry to a rodent leg. The point is, the server was obviously on their toes enough to handle the problem quickly and effectively. They managed to keep the customer satisfied. Their actions stood out in this customer's mind as special treatment. Now, in truth, we all know, that correcting a dish of bad food is not really something that is *above* and *beyond* the call of duty, but rather, something that is *expected* and *deserved*. The key words here are **"without being asked"**. That is the action that impressed the customer. That is the action that made this customer think of the server's behavior as 'special'. They are important words. It was an important action. It caused the customers 'reaction' to be one of gratitude and pleasantness. The server turned the bad situation into a good one — the old 'lemons from lemonade' method. The customer was saved — for the server, and for the establishment. Now, I am assuming the customer got a new salad which was void of unwanted guests, and that it was free. That would have been the right thing to do. You know it. The customer knows it. Management knows it. The customer remembers the server acting "without being asked" and not that they almost got a mouthful of " _ _ ? ? ?_ _ "!)

"server made wonderful selections on the menu; attentive without being obnoxious" (This customer probably means "suggestions" and not "selections". I don't know of many customers who would actually let their servers do the "selecting" of their food; but a great many customers are interested in the server's "suggestions". This server obviously made great ones. They knew their menu and facility well. Further, the server served the table attentively, but was not intrusive. Perfect balance. You see, it can be done; and people will deeply appreciate and remember it.)

"we had waited over an hour, with reservations, to be seated; the manager said that we were so nice about waiting that he wasn't going to charge us for our meal; that was great; we talk about it to everybody" (This time it was the manager who made lemons into lemonade, and what an impact it must have had on the server. Just imagine the frame of mind of this customer had the manager not acted this way. The server would have gone to the table with serious strikes against him. When customers have been subjected to unthinkable delays before you even get to them, you are serving with a tremendous handicap. It is likely that no matter what you do, you will not be able to make them forget the frustration they have already experienced just trying to get to a table. Nevertheless, if this happens you must try your very best to turn the tide. In this case, the manager did the right thing. But you will not always be able to count on management's brains or abilities. I have known many managers who would have let these people walk out the door before trying to make anything up to them. Such bad management is rampant in our 'blameless' society. Many managers would have taken the position that whatever caused the delay was someone else's fault, or beyond their control. They don't seem to understand that absolutely *nothing* that happens in their restaurant is not their fault, or to their credit, as the case may be. Absolutely *everything* is ultimately in their control. So, this server was indeed fortunate because of this manager's actions. As a result of the manager's behavior, the server faced customers who had had a miserable experience wiped from their minds by the knowledge that the meal was going to be free. Such a little thing, but oh so important. The cost of the meal was an investment in the future of this customer with this restaurant. Kudos to the managers, and to the servers, who recognize this incredibly crucial fact. The customer said, "we talk about it to everybody". Good word-of-mouth far outweighs any amount of advertising dollars.)

"after being told by the cooks that they were out of strawberries, and seeing my disappointment, the server checked for himself and found some, and brought me about a quart of them!" (I love this server. The cooks were lazy; the server was not! This customer will never forget this. I'm certain that a 'quart' is not a normal serving amount, but the restaurant deserves to pay the cost of the extra strawberries for tolerating laziness and apathy in their kitchens. As a server, you can't customarily give away food. If you do, the restaurant will collapse, and you will be unemployed. But, on certain occasions, like this one, it was the right thing to do. The customer's extreme disappointment in the establishment was averted. The server was a hero; and, the customer's reaction was one of glee. And I will bet my bottom dollar, the tip was as big as that quart of strawberries!)

"after forgetting to bring us our silverware for half of the meal (we took some from another table), he said 'dinner is on me'" (Bravo!! Bravo!! Bravo!! The server committed a grave sin, but he understood that **he was responsible for his own behavior.** A server who will pick up the check to make up for his own bad behavior is a server who will someday be among the best there ever was. The lack of silverware was forgotten by the customer. They remembered, instead, a server who made a serious mistake but who stepped up to the plate and accepted responsibility for his own actions. He didn't blame the busperson, his bunions, the weather, or anything else. The blame belonged to him and he acknowledged it and honored it. Bravo!! Bravo!! Bravo!!)

"let me go home to get my wallet" (Sometimes, it pays to have trust; sometimes it doesn't. The simple truth is this: most people are instinctively honest. We hear most about the rotten few who think the world owes them something — those who think it's just plain okay to steal. But the biggest percentage of your customers will not be among society's rotten bunch. This customer will never forget this server's trust in him. It's a judgment call, for sure. Just try to put yourself in the customer's shoes and imagine that it is an honest mistake. My husband has frequently left the house without some vital accessory – wallet, keys, phone, glasses, computer, CD's, me. . .(*arghhh*!) Yet because stuff happens, I can identify with some poor embarrassed customer who suddenly realizes his wallet has slipped out of his pocket and is sitting in his lazyboy at home. Think about it, and don't automatically assume your customer is trying to run out on the check. Something can always be worked out. When this customer returned with his wallet, I'll just bet there was a little extra something in there to show his gratitude to the server who trusted him. This server took a risk that was definitely above and beyond the call of duty and I'm sure was rewarded both financially, and spiritually, for it.)

"the server took my daughter's trout back to the kitchen, to have it de-boned" (I'm not clear on whether the actual de-boning was something the server did, or asked a cook to do. It doesn't matter. Either way, it was a gracious and accommodating thing to do - special and memorable.)

"helped me set up a nice birthday surprise for my husband; the server hid the cake and gifts until the appropriate time; then made a big fuss over my husband (it embarrassed the heck out of him, and I don't think he necessarily enjoyed it, but I loved it); I appreciated all the extra effort on the part of the server" (Here, indeed, is a server with a clue. The server made a special occasion even more special by getting into the spirit of things. Perhaps the server could have been a little more sensitive to the poor embarrassed birthday boy and toned down the fussing over him just a bit. However, this server knew who to please to make that tip grow, and obviously did just that. The server made the wife who planned this little shindig very happy indeed. Just remember, going above and beyond the call of duty to help accommodate a party, is not the same as joining in. Don't don their paper hats. Serve; don't party down. This server apparently made the right choices. Special occasions are built-in tip-boosting opportunities. Use them; just don't abuse them.)

"educated me on what wine would be nice with my meal; and it wasn't the most expensive bottle!" (Excellent! This server sent a clear message to the customer that what they cared most about was the customer's enjoyment, and not just inflating the check. A customer can't ask for more than to have a server who cares enough to put the customers' feelings first and is well-trained enough to execute and implement such caring and effective service. Caring without training, or training without caring, just doesn't cut the mustard. It takes both. And customers readily recognize the servers who have both.)

"although we were celebrating my birthday, we had not mentioned it to the server, nor did we know that the restaurant provided complimentary cakes for birthdays; the server overheard us and surprised me with a cake!" (This server listened! Oh, glory be! Excellent 'I Spy' tactics deployed. Result? A direct hit! Big tip!! The server seized the opportunity and scored. The customer was delighted and lists this as the most special dining experience of her life. A special little surprise, sincerely given, can move mountains.)

"our kids like cherries in their soft drinks and told the waitress so; one waitress brought their drinks with six or seven cherries in them; the kids loved it; I thought it was a nice touch" (How much does a cherry cost? This was definitely a good investment. This mother remembers and has probably frequented this restaurant on many subsequent occasions. Such a little thing, a few extra cherries, but so very special to the kids. Special to the kids makes it special to the mom. Servers who think on their feet must be applauded. I've said it before; free food is not the most important way to big tips, and it shouldn't be. But sometimes, especially when it is something so small, it is quite appropriate. I don't want servers do get the idea that, "hey, if I screw up, it doesn't matter as long as I slip them some free food". That is not what I am saying at all. That would be just an excuse for bad server behavior, which is unacceptable — free food or not. It is not the same thing whatsoever as gifting someone with a little surprise in response to something you have heard or observed. This server deserved a special tip for her special behavior. Besides, the surprised smiles on the kids faces just had to be worth the extra little effort.)

"brought me plenty of ice water, ice, and coffee" (Isn't this just too sad? This poor, pathetic customer thinks they have been given special, memorable treatment just because their drinks were kept properly filled. Don't you just want to weep? I do. This comment shows the deplorable state of service in this country. I mean, *really*. This is *not* service above and beyond the call of duty. This is just good service. Customers are **entitled** to good service at all times. Now, would somebody out there please do something truly special for this customer and all others like them who obviously need a loving touch? Check out your station, this customer may be sitting there — you know, the one thanking you profusely for giving them a one whole paper napkin with their rack of ribs. They are so grateful for so little.)

"insisted that she was going to pay for my meal herself because she had to take it back twice to get the meat done (which was not her fault); I didn't let her pay, but I really appreciated her offer" (Now, this really is an action above and beyond the call of duty! This server should be a manager - today. She knew the customer had been shamefully inconvenienced and sought to compensate them for that inconvenience — even though everyone knew she had not cooked the meat herself. I salute her; but it would have been a shame if she had paid the bill herself. That was the responsibility of the management. She thought like a manager. That was commendable. Ideally, she should have taken her actions one step further, and after the customer refused to let her pay for the check, apprise the manager of the situation and let him compensate the customer. As it was, the server is highly thought of by the customer, but did the restaurant fare as well? Will this customer return to an establishment where it took a cook three tries to cook some meat? Management should definitely have been told about this and given the opportunity to mitigate the damage to the restaurant's reputation. The server is well remembered, but probably not the restaurant. I believe this server will do well wherever she works. She clearly thinks about the consequences of the damage of badly prepared food. I tend to believe that she probably did tell management. It seems to be in her nature to do so. I have to wonder if management just didn't act on the information.)

"when there was supposed to be no substitutes, the server gave me a Yorkshire pudding with my entree when it was only included on another entree" (Yes, this was special treatment; but it was not special treatment that can necessarily be attributed to actions above and beyond the call of duty, but rather, to policy violation. That is a whole different kettle of fish. Now, I don't want to be too judgmental about this, because it's apparent this customer was greatly impressed, and grateful. It is an action that I can honestly say I may have taken myself. Caution: you must be extremely careful about violating restaurant policies. Frankly, I don't understand or approve of the 'no substitute' policy that many restaurants feel the need to dictate. I think a restaurant is better served by giving standard 'choices'. Those choices can most assuredly be structured so that customers would not be able to 'rob them blind' or get something for nothing. The issue is clear; if there is in existence a 'no substitute' policy, you are obligated to abide by it. There are exceptions; there are *always* exceptions to every rule. That is where good judgment comes in. This may have been one of those exceptions. With experience you will know a real exception when you see one.)

"caught us in the parking lot to bring us an item we had forgotten at the table" (I give this server a big A+. The server went above and beyond the call of duty, *after* the tip had already been left. A good server. A good human being. Salute!)

"**she took me home with her when she got off. . .but that's probably not what you're looking for here. . .**" (I love a sense of humor!!!!! This customer definitely has one. As for the server who, uh, er, welcomed him to her home, I think this may have been just a touch *too* above and beyond the call of duty.)

"**quietly observed what was needed and did it without 'asking' every time**" (That's the way! Don't bug your customers. Do as this server did, and efficiently do your job without intruding all of the time. Sometimes, it is necessary to ask questions; mostly, it isn't. Customers notice these things. You may not realize it, but they most *definitely* do.)

"**left restaurant to get something for our small child**" (I don't get it. What could possibly have been outside the restaurant suitable for a small child? Did the server gather some twigs and rocks for him to play with, or did the server jump in his car and go on a 'Pamper' run? The possibilities are puzzling. "Getting something" to keep a small child happy - that's a good thing. Deserting your other customers to do so - that's a bad thing. This server may have scored big with this customer, but I'm fairly certain the other tables in his station weren't so dadgummed happy about it! Like I said, I don't get it. I just thought I would include it to get your mind to wonder, as mine has been doing for some time now about this comment. Misery does love company you know. Well so does confusion! What is your hypothesis?)

"**I was in labor; she got my food immediately**" (You've got to be kidding! I rather think any server on the planet would have reacted the same way. Can't you just see a server saying, "Sorry, ma'am, no one gets special treatment here; you'll have to tell the baby to wait like everybody else." *Puh-leeze!*)

"**gave me a brief history of a historical establishment without being asked and kept it brief**" (Server: "Hello, my name is LuLu, and I'll be your server today. Did you know that the Queen Mary is a big ship, from England, and it's even named for a real Queen, and it even floats, and has a big anchor, and what would you like to order?" Call me thick. Call me stupid. But I don't get this one either. I'm not sure which one is the extraterrestrial — the server, or the customer! Yet lo and behold; this was one customer's most memorable server experience. Some people really ought to get out more.)

"restaurant owner made a point to make a personal comment at my daughter's birthday dinner party" (If you are lucky enough to have an owner, or manager, like this one, you have an ace up your sleeve. My favorite restaurants are the ones where I am made to feel like the most important customer on earth. Sure, I know I am not the only one. All of the customers in these types of restaurants are made to feel the same way. Receiving a kind word or inquiry from owners and managers is a big boon to the restaurant's reputation, and ultimately, its bottom line. I have found that in establishments where this is common practice, the servers naturally follow suit with their own attentiveness. Simple caring can be quite contagious. However, if your owner, or manager, is not friendly and sincere with the customers, that is no excuse for *you* to be unfriendly and insincere as well. But, boy oh boy, if they are friendly and attentive, they make your job a whole lot brighter. Read this customer's comment to your manager. Show them just how much people care about *management's* behavior.)

"had chef make special fried potatoes, the way mother used to make" (Well, if you can get your chef to go along with something like this, you had better share that big tip with him. These kinds of stories are very rare. In this day and age of assembly-line everything, it is so nice to hear something like this. This server, this cook, and this restaurant are all tops in my book as they obviously were in the customer's book. I just have one question. How did the chef know exactly how the customer's mother actually cooked her potatoes?)

"I was hitching a long time ago; had enough for coffee; stopped, and waitress chatted with me until I kind of spilled out my story; she told me to order anything on the menu, her treat" (I'd like to think that this was some time ago, like maybe the flower-power years of the sixties, when hitchhiking wasn't a lethal undertaking. Sadly, hitchhiking today is no longer one friendly stranger helping another; it's just suicide. Such is the way of serving, too. So often a server's only motivation to do a kind act is the tip. It's refreshing to hear of servers who acted so beautifully knowing there would never be a tip. If all servers could derive pleasure from being a giving person, and act out of simple kindness, it would be amazing how wonderful we all would feel. It would feel like living on a rainbow. I'm sure this waitress realizes a great reward in big tips, but even if she didn't, she would still treat her customers the same. Such is the ideal server — caring about the customer, caring about themselves, and letting the tips blossom naturally, the way they will when nurtured properly. A customer can spot a phony, someone smiling falsely hoping for a big tip, or someone who appears to be solicitous when they are really quite the opposite. The kind of server mentioned by this customer is the kind that shines in everyone's eyes, and hearts, and wallets.)

"I was having a very long wait waiting on a business associate to arrive and join me; the server noticed and bought me a newspaper and brought it to me" (Brilliant! This is probably the best twenty-five cent investment I have ever heard of. What an impression this server made with such a small but generous act!)

"the server treated my elderly aunt who has Alzheimer's, like a long lost friend; my aunt loved her, and we did too" (Compassion and understanding — what a concept. This server took a possibly awkward situation and made the best of it. This customer will never forget this server. It was a win-win situation for everybody. That's the ticket - "win-win".)

"the hostess (and cashier) recognizes me and gives me the senior discount every time I come in even though I'm not a senior" (This is beautiful. Someone at that restaurant understands loyalty and rewards it appropriately. That five or ten percent given to this regular customer keeps him, or her, coming back and makes the servers' jobs so much easier. Loyalty should always be rewarded. If management does not know the regulars, someone should. In this instance, it is clear that the customer repeatedly patronizes this establishment, and the hostess/cashier took it upon themselves to say 'thank you' on behalf of the restaurant. Good thinking. I'd say this employee is definitely management material. It was not done for any personal gain. The hostess/cashier never gets tips. It was done for the gain of everyone - from the customer, to the server, to the restaurant itself. A classic "win-win". Exceptional work. The servers in this restaurant are lucky to have this hostess/cashier on their side.)

"**the server always brings me a carafe of iced tea even though it is not a customary procedure in the restaurant**" (I like this one. I like it a lot. Why? It's very personal to me. I **hate** to wait for my iced tea to be replenished. When I want it, I want it. I don't want it at someone else's convenience. An avid iced tea drinker is more than happy to pour their own. A pitcher or carafe of iced tea is a blessing to the customer and a time-saver for the server. As you can see, it makes the customer remember, and, feel special. I just don't understand why more don't use this simple remedy to a very common problem. This server would get bonus points, and a fatter tip, from me.)

"**dinner reservations for 8:00; never got seated until 9:15; waiter gave us special attention and service, very sympathetic, and dessert and coffee was 'on the house'**" (When the management doesn't rectify such an inexcusable delay, the server must do all in their power to do so. This server did just that. The coffee and dessert was a good save. The customer remembered this evening well. The times were impressed in their minds. They remembered that they waited and waited and waited to be seated, but they also remembered that the server picked up the dropped ball and made the touchdown. This server understands that whatever caused the delay, it most certainly wasn't the customer's fault, and they should not have to suffer for it. If the host or management slips, pick up the slack.)

"**offered to change one item of food for another in a very friendly manner**" (See how easy it can be? Every special request doesn't have to be a major ordeal. Just go with it. If you want your tips to improve, you must accommodate your customers needs and desires above and beyond the call of duty. There are many tiny little ways to do that. This is one of them.)

"when the waiter came to the table and said 'how is everyone today?', I casually replied that I had a headache; when he brought the drinks, the waiter also brought me a towel with ice in it for my headache" (This is my favorite response! I give this waiter 4 stars for compassion; 4 stars for listening; 4 stars for ingenuity; 4 stars for remedy; and a big 4 stars for having the good sense to be a food server. The industry needs him! If I knew who he was, I'd send him a twenty-dollar bill myself!)

Something very important to remember here is that the responses you have just read were to the question, "describe something special a server did for you that you will never forget". I did not ask: "what was the best service you ever received?" There is a difference. The responses above relate to *one* special stand-out event during a dining experience. "The best service ever received" would have been described as a service free from bad server behaviors, *as well as* a special stand-out event the server did. You will not always have the opportunity to benefit from one special event alone. Your ordinary standards of service must be extremely high if you want to make big money in food service. Customers are deeply impressed with overall excellence. These special behaviors we have just heard about are just the icing on the cake. To be the best server in town, you must develop a solid foundation of good work habits, be incredibly organized, then top it off by giving special attention to each and every customer. Amazingly, it's not that hard to accomplish.

One final note here: this question, asking the customer to describe their most memorable dining experience, was left blank on the questionnaires more often than any other. How sad.

Question 8:

This question was simple. I asked the customers to "describe the one thing you care most about in food service". Their 'not-so-surprising' responses included:

"**cleanliness and neatness**" (Told you so; told you so. This was the most frequent response to this question. No surprise here.)
"**food must be served hot and served at one time otherwise some of a party might be finished before others are served**" (You betcha!)
"**courtesy and knowledge**" (Without a doubt!)
"**friendliness of server; a clean restaurant**" (All employees must work together to see that these are normal circumstances, not rare ones.)
"**good food with prompt service from a clean server**" (In a nutshell!)
"**clean, attentive, personable**" (Same strokes from different folks.)
"**good food, correctly cooked, reasonably priced and served promptly**" (It never hurts to hear it again and again.)
"**food done to my taste exactly; clean silverware, clean, prompt server; and an enjoyable atmosphere - calm, quiet, peaceful, attractive environment with soothing music and interesting decor**" (Ambiance - it's so very important, whether it's a roadside diner or a fancy restaurant, it matters. As to the music, I wholeheartedly agree. I protest to the management anytime I am subjected to rock music during my meal. Unless I choose to eat at the Hardrock Cafe, or some equally rock 'n' roll-oriented establishment, I do not want to be blasted with music I would never choose on my own. Unless it is a theme or ethnic restaurant, music should be neutral and in the background where it belongs. I am equally disturbed by a restaurant with no music at all. Who wants to hear people munching, crunching, slurping and burping?!)
"**a server with a good attitude**" (Absolutely!)
"**quality, intelligent, capable, server**" (Like I said, a solid foundation, extreme organization, and a special attentiveness. These are the keys!)

"speedy and efficient service done with courtesy and cheerfulness" (Sound familiar?)
"politeness" (Please and thank you very much.)
"waiters and waitresses who are nice to my kids; not condescending, but truly nice" (Kids are people, too! Their parents are the tippers!)
"pleasant atmosphere; server who loves his/her job; excellent food; makes me feel I'm special (I am)" (This customer defines it beautifully. I couldn't have said it better myself!)
"courtesy and friendliness; the restaurants we frequent have servers that acknowledge our loyalty and act as though they're genuinely happy to see us (we've noticed that the turnover of servers is low at these establishments, too)" (I can understand why.)
"quality and persistence - stay with me and I'll treat you right (I'm a picky customer, but I tip very well if the server does it right)" (Remember what I told you - please the most demanding customer and the rest are a walk in the park.)
"a cheerful disposition; I like to feel welcomed when I dine out; I dislike a server who makes me feel like I am inconveniencing them; I can even overlook slow service if the atmosphere and the server is pleasant" (Not many of your customers would be this forgiving of slow service; but it does show you how important a pleasant personality is to your job. It's not the only requirement, by far, but it is very, *very* important to good tips.)
"a smoke-free environment" (Me, too. Smoke on food is repulsive and sick. [Smokers may disagree with this.] Fortunately, I live in California where all restaurants are smoke-free. What a joy!)
"a server who understands my order" (I'm not sure if the customer is talking about a good listener, a person of reasonable intelligence, or one who speaks fluent English. Since all three are vital, it doesn't matter. They all need to be part of a server's better qualities.)
"style and class" (Amen.)

The responses to this question had numerous repeats, the top contenders being: cleanliness (of server and restaurant), promptness, hot food, good food, good attitude and personality, and smoke-free dining. Is that so much to ask? I think not.

Question 9:

Question 9 dealt with comments and observations that the customers felt would make food service better. The responses were broad, some offering suggestions for the restaurant itself, some for the servers, some for management, and even some for the customers. Many answers to this question were repetitions of views we've already discussed elsewhere; but here are a few of your customers' more creative suggestions:

"**coffee and dessert go together, servers should remember to inquire about coffee**" (Not for me. I hate coffee. But I understand their point.)

"**don't come around to remove food when you can see I'm still eating**" ("I Spy" eyes!)

"**make sure the air conditioning doesn't bother the diners, like being too cold; either change the tables or turn it down**" (Shivering or boiling customers won't come back!)

"**when I go out to eat, I go to enjoy the food and the company of my companions, not to become buddies with my waiter or waitress; they should take care of people without interrupting them**" (I wholeheartedly concur.)

"**servers should wear a uniform or some outfit that distinguishes them, other than just an apron**" (Crisp, clean uniforms are impressive and set a tone.)

"**establishments should spend quality time in training the staff in food preparation and service**" (Amen and hallelujah!)

"**the food should have to pass 'good taste' tests**" (Not everyone's tastes are the same, but we hope that the chefs do taste their own cooking.)

"**servers should earn better pay**" (Don't you just love this one!!)

"**restaurants should have enough help so the servers aren't tripping over themselves trying to wait on more tables than they can handle" (Say it again — Amen!)

"I know they are busy, but a bit of friendly chit chat is nice when it happens, but not when I'm eating, though" (Friendly and brief; brief and friendly.)

"free dessert if the food is not served within a certain time" (Gotta' love it!)

"restaurants should concentrate on training and hiring experienced servers with references; more servers at busy establishments so less tables per server" (Customers apparently think alike!)

"control the temperatures of the table areas better" (Comfort for the customers before comfort for the workers!)

"acknowledge exceptional service with recognition awards to help servers want to improve" (I second the motion.)

"have servers who do the 'best that they can do' and be pleasant about it; I'll be pleasant too" (Isn't that nice.)

"continue to make the public aware through newspaper publication the ratings of the various eating places that fail to meet the standards of the Public Health Department" (I like it.)

"keep everything clean - silverware; glassware; plates and dishes; chairs; floors; servers, etc." (Yes, yes, yes!)

"employ servers with good attitudes" (Hire only the pick of the litter.)

"hire people who really want to be food servers and who know how to be one" (Caring and training; training and caring. One without the other won't cut the mustard!)

"have all restaurants be non-smoking; it's awful when you sit in the non-smoking section and you leave with your clothes smelling of cigarette smoke" (My vote, as well as my fellow Californian's votes, counted. In California, *all* restaurants are now smoke-free!)

"for customers eating later in day, do not serve warmed up food or pour last of coffee in pot in our cups" (Every customer is just as important as the first customer of the day!)

"make the servers be polite or get fired" (Without a doubt!)

"never use cleaners that smell while customers are eating in restaurant" (ABSOLUTELY!)

"offer healthy children's menus, not just hot dogs, etc." (Really, we are killing our kids.)

"strive to be the best restaurant ever" (That should do it!)

And now, for the answer to the question you have all been waiting for...

Question 10:

The question: "What percentage of the check is your customary tip?
The answer:

% of respondents	customary tip
42%	15%
24%	20%
12%	15-20%
12%	10%
6%	10-15%
2%	15-18%
2%	20-30%

What we can readily determine from the above statistics is that an enormous **82%** of your customers routinely tip **15%** or better. Most importantly, **100%** of your customers **do** tip. In fairness, I will tell you that I received 2 surveys that were not figured in to the above percentages. One of those tipped 5%; and one tipped a whopping 3%. Because they were just one survey each, their percentage calculates to zero percent of the total number of surveys. I am telling you about them because you are already aware that once in a very blue moon, you will get a big spender like this who will not tip you any better for better service. But the surveys prove, beyond the shadow of a doubt, what I've already said — these people are inconsequential in numbers and are definitely *not* typical restaurant patrons. Besides, you don't know who they are in advance, so the rule of thumb is: superior service to all!

How do your tips measure up to the averages here? We'll delve more into that later as we discuss your Business Diary.

Question 11:
Question: "Do you tip more (a larger percentage) at fine dining establishments than you do at diners or chain restaurants?"
Answer: 51% - NO
            49% - YES

(This is truly a split decision, but it shows that those working in diners have as much opportunity as those in fine-dining houses to earn the maximum tips.)

Question 12:
Question: "Do you expect the servers to be better at fine dining establishments than at diners?"
Answer: 77% - YES
            23% - NO

(This is unacceptable! All servers have the ability to be wonderful regardless of where they are employed! This is one perception that all servers should strive to change!)

And now, a drumroll please. . . . .

Question 13:
Question: "If you receive exceptional service, do you tip more than your customary percentage?"
Answer: 96% - YES
             2% - Sometimes (write-ins)
             2% - NO

(Is this eye-opening, or what?! <u>96%</u> will tip you better if you perform better! What a great and easy way to give yourself a nice big fat raise!)

Question 14:

Question: "Name an example of what you consider to be exceptional service."

I will only mention a few of the responses here as so many are repetitions of the points we have already digested.

"**explain to customer, if asked, what they think is especially good on the menu and then check on order to see if it is as specified and if the customer likes it**" (Be helpful!)
"**quick, courteous and correct**" (Oh, yes!)
"**exceptional service is when everything runs smoothly; service is quick and efficient; the food is excellent; and the server is attentive but not bothersome**" (Sums it up don't you think?)
"**remembering to refill**" (Such a little thing to be thought of as exceptional!)
"**having a server and establishment who will honor the needs of my restricted diet**" (It's important.)
"**one who anticipates one's needs**" (Organization!!!!)
"**when you order something and you realize after you get it that it was not what you thought it was and they take it back and let you reorder**" (Sometimes menus are misleading.)
"**waiters and waitresses who look and act like professionals**" (You *are* professionals!)
"**correcting problems instantaneously**" (Waiting is a drag.)
"**prompt, courteous service even in a crowded restaurant**" (Crowded or not, it's vital!)
"**clean, friendly, helpful servers who are responsive to my needs**" (People wouldn't have to wish for this type of server if more servers were this kind. . .)

What is so interesting about the responses to the above question? What is the general theme? It's so obvious — all people want are the **simple** things. If you notice, there is not one single stand-out answer to what people view as *exceptional* service. Not one. Of all of the surveys, there was not one single response to **Question 14** that described any act I consider to be exceptional service. The comments mentioned here merely describe the type of service that should be considered ordinary, not extraordinary! All of you out there are being let off so easy! There is not one response here that you shouldn't live up to every single day of your job. That shows us the state of expectation in our society. We are so accustomed to **BAD** service that we have come to view ordinary good service as **exceptional**! How sad for society. But what an opportunity for *you*! Now just imagine for a moment, that you truly *do* conduct yourself in a manner that is without a doubt, exceptional. Why, your customers would be so amazed and stunned they just might hand over the keys to their Mercedes! Yippee!

The answers I received to this question clearly show you that the sky is the limit for your tips. It is within your power to stand out from the crowd of run-of-the-mill servers and shine like a bright glistening magnet — a magnet just plastered with the big fat tips it has attracted. Hey, go for it! Just do it! Be exceptional and wow the socks off 'em!

Refer again to **Question 13**. Do you get the drift? A mind-blowing **96%** of your customers stated that without fail they tip more than their usual percentage for exceptional service. They tip **MORE!!!!** And because, as we now realize, their expectations of the kind of service they will receive is relatively low, your opportunities are endless. If you fail to capitalize on them, it is no one's fault but your own. Remember, accept responsibility for your own actions. Once you realize that it is *you*, and you alone, who is responsible for the amount of money you make, you will begin to rise above your ordinary self and excel as you never have before!

Question 15:

Question 15 asked our respondents to name an example of server behavior they consider to be absolutely **intolerable** and **unacceptable**. These answers should surprise no one.

"placing dropped silverware or dishes back on the table"
"rudeness'
"gossiping with co-workers about management or other workers
    within hearing distance of my table"
"going on break while you wait"

"chewing gum"
"ignoring me"
"smoking within view of customers"
"impatience"
"eating in view of me"
"making multiple mistakes on the check"
"being dirty or sick" (by far, the biggest response)
"throwing the food down"
"waiting on people who came in after I did"
"being slow and lazy"
"crabbiness"
"disappearing acts"
"sloppiness"
"arrogance or snobbiness"
"not making eye contact with customer"
"too long of waiting time"
"treating my kids as second-class"
"telling me things that I have no interest in"
"bad body odor"
"doesn't listen to me"
"cares more about the tip than me"

We've heard them all before, but they just can't be reiterated enough. I hope that the more you see it, the more it will soak in. The dining customers who completed these surveys have experienced these things over and over and over again, or they wouldn't be cropping up so frequently. I am not surprised. As a customer, I have been the recipient of all of these things myself. As a server, I have observed them being performed more times than I could ever remember. But I am very dismayed to know, and you should be equally dismayed to learn, that they are not isolated incidents. They are not confined to just one type of establishment, or one locale. Rather, they are like a cancer, spread throughout our dining society — growing and multiplying until they destroy what they are part of. It doesn't have to be that way. It absolutely should not be that way. You can change it; and when you do, everyone will reap the rewards. You will be less tired and make more money. Your customers will receive better service and be happier. And your establishment will gain a reputation that will make their own bottom line bloom. Win-win-win!

Question 16:

In **Question 16**, the respondents were simply asked to indicate a Yes or No answer to whether or not they were bothered by certain specific server behaviors. This final question sums up all of the answers that have gone before it in a way that should, once and for all, stop you from ever doing these things.

"Does it bother you to see your server. . . . ."

. . .talking with other servers when you need them?
> 83% - **YES**
> 17% - NO

. . .sitting down while you are their customer?
> 51% - **YES**
> 49% - NO

. . .smoking in view of customers?
> 81% - **YES**
> 19% - NO

(NOTE: of the 19% who said that seeing their server smoking does not bother them, 80% of those respondents were smokers themselves. That means that of the non-smokers who completed the surveys, **96%** of them were bothered to see their server smoking. Interestingly, even 20% of the smokers who answered this question, were themselves bothered by seeing their server smoke. Remember, as a rule, non-smokers are *more demanding* [holding the server to a *higher standard of conduct*] than smokers.)

...eating in view of customers?
    57% - YES
    43% - NO

(NOTE: of the 43% here who said that seeing their server eating *does not* bother them, 75% of the respondents were smokers. Of the non-smokers who completed the surveys, **83%** *were* bothered to see their server eating in view of the customers; aka: demanding a *higher standard of conduct* which you must *exceed* to attain optimum tips)

...chatting about personal matters with other customers when you are trying to get their attention?
    85% - **YES**
    15% - **NO**

...ignoring dirty dishes on your table?
    74% - **YES**
    26% - **NO**

...running around frantically?
    43% - **YES**
    57% - **NO**

...leaving in the middle of your service?
    85% - **YES**
    15% - **NO**

...carrying too many plates and dishes at once?
    34% - **YES**
    66% - **NO**

...moving like a snail?
    85% - **YES**
    15% - **NO**

...being a pest by bothering you too much?
    70% - **YES**
    30% - **NO**

...treating other customers differently than you?
    77% - **YES**
    23% - **NO**

The conclusions may surprise you. I was certainly surprised by some of the responses. For example, it seems that a majority of your customers are inclined to forgive your Packmule and Roadrunner actions. They indicated by their responses that those two things did not bother them as much as other things. The important point to remember, however, is that of even these two behaviors, **34% were genuinely bothered** by the Packmule behavior and **43% were genuinely bothered** by Roadrunners. While in the minority, those are still **significant** numbers. As I have stated repeatedly, if you want to make big tips, you must please the most exacting of customers. If you do, the rest will be a snap. I should mention that a good number of the respondents wrote comments along side their "Yes" or "No" responses. Regarding "running around frantically" (one of the Roadrunner behaviors), and, "carrying too many plates and dishes at once" (one of the Packmule behaviors), a substantial number of the "NO" responses were qualified with a notation that said **"if they are really busy"**. This clearly indicates that those customers would not be so forgiving of those behaviors when it appears that the restaurant is not all that crowded. Those little qualifications are important to note.

Another interesting response to me was that 26% of the respondents weren't overly bothered by dirty dishes on their table. Well blow me over with a feather! I am astounded! Your dining public is far more generous with you than you deserve. Dirty dishes should always be removed promptly. I wonder if this 26% cleans up after their own meals at home? Just a thought. But the important fact is that a huge **74% *are* bothered** by it, and justly so.

Clearly the most offensive behaviors from this list proved to be:

- talking with other servers when you need them
- smoking in view of customers
- chatting about personal matters with other customers when you are trying to get their attention
- leaving in the middle of your service
- moving like a snail

All twelve behaviors described in this question, (as well as all other bad behaviors mentioned throughout the survey), should absolutely be eliminated from your work habits if you want to maximize your tips. While some of them are clearly more offensive than others, they are all bad. **They all cost you money.**

****

And there you have it. The survey responses are complete. Your customers have spoken. Have you listened? Did your own answers to the survey match those answers of your customers? Are you aware of what your customers are looking for in a server? Have you realized just how vital your appearance, behavior, and organization are to your customer? Have you willingly accepted that you can improve? Have you honestly accepted responsibility for your own success? If you have answered "Yes" to all of these questions, then you are well on your way to bigger money and a happier work environment.

So let's make it personal, and talk about a way to zero in on your own areas of failure, and, excellence.

Chapter Six

DEAR DIARY

PERSONAL, PRIVATE, AND PROSPEROUS!

Have you ever tracked your own statistics? You should. You are a business. All good businesses maintain records and statistics. As a server, you are not just somebody's employee; you are indeed a small business. Why? If you control the profits, which you do, then you are a business. Now that you realize you are a business; begin to act like one. It's not enough to just count your tips at the end of the shift and cry "Yahoo!", or "Bah Humbug!". If you want to improve your tips, you must know exactly how you are doing. You must be diligent in your efforts to pinpoint just what your problems are, and what is causing them. There is one very effective way to do that. It is the gospel of all good business: Document, Document, Document! The maintaining of detailed and complete records underscores every successful business on earth. You must do the same if you want to be a truly successful business. Here's how:

At work, keep a small notepad in your pocket. On it, put the date, hours of shift and three columns, titled: "Check Amount"; "Tip Amount"; "Number in Party". When you retrieve your tip, take just a second of your time and jot down the appropriate information in each column. (Do not do this in view of your customers, please.) Later, at home, grab your calculator (or pencil and brain power) and determine your percentages. How many tables tipped 10%, 15%, 20%, or other? Are you getting tipped above or below the statistics listed by your customers in the survey? Are you doing worse, or better, or right about average? Don't get confused. Naturally, if the check is larger, so is the tip. That is not what we are talking about here. We are talking about *percentages*. We are talking about the percentage of the check you receive in a tip. The size of the check itself is irrelevant; it's unimportant information. What *is* important, is the percentage of the check that you get to take home — your tip. If your check amount is $17.50 (before the sales tax is added), and you received a tip of $2.00, what is that percentage? Divide $2.00 by $17.50 and you will see that you received only about an 11% tip. That two dollars doesn't look so great now, does it? Not when the majority of the customers are tipping over 15% as their usual, ordinary tip. It is the *percentage* that is important to you. Those percentage records are what becomes your barometer for measuring your financial success.

Next, look at the number of people in each party. Do you see any patterns forming? Do you get tipped a bigger percentage for smaller tables? If so, you may have a problem handling larger parties and need to work harder on your organizational skills. Do your percentages hold true for all size tables? You must compare apples to apples, not apples to oranges. Remember, it is the **percentage**, not the size of the check, that matters.

Once you have gleaned the statistical information from the data on your notepad, transfer that information onto a log you will keep at home. Be very specific in your log. It should contain significantly greater detail than your notepad. For example, you should create columns on the log where you will keep track of your statistical information from your notepad. Additionally, you will note the day of the week, the date, the total number of tables for your shift, your appearance, your mistakes, and your mental and physical well-being. There should also be a diary section for notes.

Record how you felt that day, both physically, and mentally. Did you go to work with a headache? Where you particularly worried about something that day? Did you have any problems at work? Was your stress level out of control? All of this information is very important to you. How can you hope to improve and increase your tips if you don't know why they are what they are now? Honest, self-examination is the first crucial step to bigger money. It is not enough to write that you were "grumpy". You must delve into the *reasons* you were grumpy. It is a common occurrence for us humans to spread our ill-content around. That's a shame; but true. If we pinpoint the single reason for our unhappiness, then we can put it in perspective and keep it from invading our every thought and action.

For those of you who have kept diaries at some point in your life, this will be easier to stick to. For those who could never seem to keep a diary, it will require more discipline. Easy or hard, you must do it. It will help you. If you choose not to help yourself, there is nothing anyone can do for you.

For your sake, and the sake of your customers and establishment, I hope you will try.

Following, are samples of what your notepad, and diary log, may look like. . .

SERVER PERSONAL RECORD

day:	date:	shift hours:
Check Amount	Tip Amount	Number In Party

(Pocket-size notepads are for pockets. Never be without it!)

TIPS

Server Diary Daily Log

date: _____ day: _____ shift hours: _____ holiday? Yes ____ No ____

Table Reference	Number in Party	Check Amount	Tip Amount	Tip Percentage	Unusual Events	Table Notes
				%		
				%		
				%		
				%		
				%		
				%		
				%		
				%		
				%		
				%		
				%		
				%		

Appearance: (early day) _____ (end of day) _____

Physical feelings: _____

Emotional feelings: _____

Thoughts: _____

TOTALS: Total day's check amounts: $ _____ Total day's tip total: $ _____ Day's percentage average: _____ %

Keeping your statistics, feelings, and notations on paper (or in your computer) will eventually make you grow. Things will start to jump out at you. Patterns will begin to emerge. This type of self-examination is priceless. If you will only pay attention, your job performance will improve. Your tips will soar. Unlike other small businesses who require professional help, like accountants or marketing directors, to interpret and analyze their data, you will not need anyone else to interpret your statistics for you. The only requirement is that you be brutally honest with yourself. If you are, then your shortcomings will be as plain as the nose on your face as you look at your own records over time.

You must keep your records religiously. It doesn't take that long once you find your rhythm. No matter how tired or rushed you are after your shift, you must take the necessary moments to record all of your day's information. Let nothing short of life-threatening emergencies get in your way. Exercise discipline. There is no need to take the time to review or try to analyze your data on a daily basis. In fact, it is unwise to do so. Simply record the information. Then once a month, set aside adequate time to really review and reflect on what appears before you. Finally, the only other step you must take, is the implementation of new and better actions which are based on what your personal logs have told you. Be receptive to your own enlightenment. Do so, and you will be surprised at how your income will start to rise and how much happier you will be — every single day you work.

Record it. Review it. Rework it. Reap the rewards! Simple.

Chapter Seven

QUICKIES

Magical Money Motivators!

In every instance of food service, there are a few standard situations that will always be present. The actions relative to these occasions should be so ingrained as to be subconscious. These situations are inborn opportunities to shine and sparkle. Here is a look at some quick and easy ways to guarantee customer delight. You may be positively astounded at how obvious they are, and at how often, in your own experience, you have seen them be ignored — either by yourself, or, your co-workers. Use them to your advantage. They exist every day and they will rocket your tips into the stratosphere!

Dapper Dialogue

I have heard so many bizarre comments from the lips of servers that I felt the need to cover the subject of "words" here. From the greeting to the good-bye, words can be very good to you; or, they can destroy you. They can fatten your bank account and soothe your spirits — but only if spoken properly and delivered meaningfully.

What's in a word? Plenty. Words convey our thoughts, our intentions, our feelings. Words themselves are generally not harmful, but when combined with a tone, an attitude, and a gesture, their meaning is deeply affected. They become powerful tools if used properly, or weapons if used maliciously, or garbage if used wastefully. Think of your dog.

If you call Fido a stupid, lazy, piece of canine offal, while holding your body in a masterful, rigid pose, with a frowning face, and a tone of voice that is angry or menacing, he will cower and be dismayed and submissive. But if you call him a stupid, lazy, piece of canine offal, in a baby-talk tone of voice, with a smile on your face, while leaning down to scratch his ears, he will think you have just praised him lavishly and be as happy as clam. The words are exactly the same, but they have been delivered in two entirely different manners. People react much the same way to the performance of words. The only difference is that people (at least most people) will also know the meaning of the words themselves. It is your responsibility to convey only what you *intend* to convey, by both word and manner.

If you say, "Have a nice day" to your customers as they are leaving, but your body language says, *"Get your sorry self out of my station!"*, well, your words have been wasted; and worse, your true message has been received by your customers. This is no way to improve tips.

Certain words and certain body language should be your subconscious workday staple. The words and phrases that are a must for your arsenal of verbal tools are the obvious ones: Sir, Ma'am, Please, Thank-You, May I, Excuse Me, Pardon Me, I'm Sorry, Allow Me, Enjoy, Hello, Hi, I Hope, I Will, My Name Is, My Pleasure, and any other word that conveys **helpfulness**, **sincerity**, and **comfort**. The body language that should accompany these words is any that is positive: a genuine smile, eye contact, relaxed posture, smooth gestures. Gentle words won't help if you look as if a broom has been stuck up your spine (or other parts of your anatomy). Frowns are your enemy. It is *absolutely possible* to smile through the worst of situations. As a bonus, a heartfelt smile can go a long way in minimizing the seriousness of any problem. Hope, faith, and optimism can indeed move mountains.

Be positive. Be sincere. Speak clearly and use polite words. Most importantly, match your body language to those words so that they are never wasted, or worse, recognized by your customers as phony. Tips can quickly be improved by applying this simple communication formula: upbeat words + upbeat demeanor = happier customers & bigger tips.

Condiment Caboodle

Here is a group of your buddies — the condiments. Yep, good old mustard, catsup, steak sauce, jam, syrup, hot sauce, dressing, relishes, etc. They are your friends. I know you're not particularly fond of them. They are a nuisance most of the time and they represent extra, seemingly unrewarded, work. But that's not the big picture. They do indeed offer reward. Why, they are no different than an adorable little baby — precious and messy.

Like a newborn, condiments demand a great deal of your attention.

Cleaning them, like changing a newborn, is not all it's cracked up to be. Caring for a newborn, and caring for a bunch of silly condiments is more alike than you think. Both jobs sometimes feel quite yukky and thankless. However, if you ignore a newborn, and don't give it the attention it deserves, you will miss out on miracle moments of joy. That joy makes the constant attention and hard work worth every effort. And if you ignore your condiments, you are missing out on one of the easiest and quickest ways to improve your tips — a joy you can definitely live with.

Clean, full condiments are so darn easy to achieve. Yet, it is amazing how horribly some of them get presented to the customers. It's such a little thing, but customers notice. Messy, or partially-full, condiments send the message that the server just doesn't care. So very many servers just plain miss this blessed opportunity to impress their customers.

Sparkling containers with no drips or spills or stains are the ticket. Don't be lazy. Don't swipe condiments from another table and deliver them to your customers without first taking them to the bus station and giving them a quick but thorough once over. Don't let management deprive you of enough containers or bottles for all servers to be able to do the job properly. Pristine condiments are effective tip boosters. They not only make the dining experience more pleasant, but they send that all important message that you, and your restaurant, are conscientious and caring.

Get into the habit of creating and serving only terrific looking condiments. Make it a subconscious part of your day. A minute here, a minute there, and you will never be put in the position of disappointing and turning off your customers. They *will* notice. They care; so if you want your tips to blossom, you must care too.

Clean, full condiments — what a concept — what an easy and quick way to better tips.

Water, Water Everywhere And Nary A Drop To Drink

Imagine you are on the back of a camel. It's been three days of nothing but sand and dust and wind. You're parched. Your lips are cracked and split. The hot sand is imbedded in every pore in your body, and you're so thirsty you wish you could shed a tear just for a drop of liquid. You've been plodding day after day after day when suddenly before you is the most beautiful oasis you have ever seen — sparkling blue water gently lapping a lush green shore. It feels so near you can almost taste it. Before you is all the water you could ever want. But wait! Between you and that thirst-quenching pool is still miles of sand. And woe is you. Your camel has just plopped himself on the ground for an afternoon snooze, refusing to budge. You know you'll never make it on your own. You need that camel. But alas, since he carries his own water, he's not thirsty. He doesn't particularly need *you*. So there you have it. The water you so desperately need and want is just out of your reach, but your camel simply isn't motivated to get you to it. How utterly miserable!

Well, my friends, you are the camel. When your customers are sitting with empty glasses or cups, be it water, iced tea, coffee, soda, or whatever your pleasure, the agony is the same. Empty glasses and cups reduce tips. Full ones promote bigger tips. Your customers are aware, that like the oasis, there is plenty to be had, if only the camel would cooperate. The restaurant hasn't suddenly gone dry, so it has to be the fault of the server. (You blasted camel you!) Keeping drinks plentiful is such a simple tip motivator. Your customers exclaim this loud and clear, by word or look or deed. All you must do is listen, observe, and respond. Replenishing drinks is a lightning way to better money. Watch those glasses and cups. Anticipate their beverage needs before they actually become needs and fill-er-up!

Do yourself a favor, and utilize this simple method of improvement. Don't let your customers go dry unless you want your tips to dry up too. After all, liquids are the body's lifeblood just as your tips are your financial lifeblood. Quick and easy. Water, water everywhere, and plenty for me to drink! Do it.

Shine, <u>Underline</u>, Shine

When a writer wants you to really pay attention to a point they are making, what do they do? They highlight it. How? In addition to using strong punctuation, like exclamation points, they may make the word or phrase **bold**, or they may *italicize* it, or they may <u>underline</u> it. If the point is monumental in importance, they may do ***<u>all of the above!</u>*** These actions are effective methods of driving the point home to the reader. Such emphasis is a writer's tool. The use of the tool draws special attention and makes a dramatic impression. This same tool is available to you as a food server.

How so? It is the simple and consistent use of underliners. More butter pats? <u>Underline</u> it! More creamers? <u>Underline</u> it! Sweating iced drinks? <u>Underline</u> it! New spoon? <u>Underline</u> it! The object is to touch as little as possible in view of your customers. Your hands are touching the underliners, not the food or object that is being served. It doesn't matter that when you went to the kitchen or bus station to get those extra pats of butter, that you grabbed them with your hand to put them on your underliner. Such an act is occurring beyond your customer's view. But if you then just hurry on over to the table and drop them off, without the use of an appropriate underliner, you have missed a golden opportunity to impress your customers — to stand out — to highlight your performance — to make the point that your service is special — to **<u>underline</u>** your abilities in their minds.

Any time you can take an action that will set the standard by which customers will judge all other servers, you are winning the race. The use of <u>underliners</u>, whether bowls, saucers, plates, coasters, or even napkins, is *your* tool of **emphasis**. It highlights your abilities and makes your service classier and more stylish. The prettier the underliner, the better it serves you. Take a clue from the chefs. Why do they put that lettuce leaf under the cottage cheese? Even though it is food, rarely does anyone ever eat the lettuce leaf. It's purpose is not to be a bonus food; its purpose is eyeball appeal. The chef's use of the lettuce leaf makes the cottage cheese stand out against an attractive, contrasting background. It makes that cottage cheese look downright inviting — a far preferable presentation than just a clump of white cottage cheese on a white plate, which, in a word, is *b-o-r-i-n-g*. It is possible to make anything you serve look better. Do it. You are not prohibited from beautifying the items you serve.

An important philosophy that will make your tips bloom is this: dining out should be a **total** experience, one that pleases *all* of the senses, not just the tastebuds or growling stomach. The six senses of dining are: seeing, smelling, hearing, touching, tasting, and feeling. Satisfy all of them, and watch your tips grow. The **eyes** should see attractively presented food, pleasant decor, and a clean and neat server. The **nose** should smell the mouthwatering aroma of fresh cooking . The **ears** should hear soothing music conducive to eating and the pleasant voice of their server. The **hands** should touch only pristinely served objects. The **tongue** should taste tantalizingly delicious morsels. The **soul** should be peaceful and content and free from any server or restaurant-caused distress. Amazingly, the simple use of attractive underliners addresses four of these six senses right off the bat — seeing, touching, tasting and feeling. It is, therefore, not difficult to recognize the importance of an act that satisfies over half of the six senses. Food that looks better has a psychological impact on the taste of the food. Further, items served in a more appealing manner contribute to the overall serene emotional state of the diner. Underliners make a subtle, and yet incredible impact. So many servers miss this great tip boat.

Using attractive underliners is smart business — for you, and for your restaurant. It's an opportunity for your service to shine and sparkle; and it's so easy to do.

Be **bold**; *stand out*; underline it!

Check It Out

Remember that infamous saying, "The job is never over until the paperwork is done`"? It's true. Even for you. The check is your paperwork. Your customers are your auditors. They will have to handle it. They will examine the check you provide because it applies directly to them. The check may seem inconsequential to you and may not even seem like part of the service. **It is very much an important part of the**

service. We talked earlier about wet checks (when a customer wrote how much they hated checks left in puddles). That was just one of the no-no's relating to checks.

The check offers another of those built-in opportunities for improved tips. Is it legible? Clean? Dry? Absolutely correct? It must be all of these things. Give the check the importance it deserves. Place it in an unobtrusive, clean, dry spot on the table. (This applies with or without a tip tray.) Always leave a pen with credit card transactions. Be attentive to when the customer would like to *receive* the check (giving the check to your customer is always your responsibility). Be attentive to when they would like to *pay* the check (if it is your responsibility to accept the payment). Customers forced to **question** or **recalculate** the check, **dry off** the check, **wipe off** the check, or **hunt you down** to get the check or pay the check, will be left with a bad impression. Even if you were brilliant in all areas up to that point, you can blow it all with poor check performance. *Or*, you can put the icing on the performance cake with excellent check presentation!

The job is truly never done until the paperwork is completed. The check is an opportunity for you to leave one last spectacular impression. It takes very little effort for the check to be presented and transacted perfectly. A little extra attention to the check will pay off in your tips. Another quick and easy way to bigger and better money! How could you possibly ignore it?

Go With It

Horse and carriage. Peanut butter and jelly. Nuts and bolts. We shall call these "go withs". One fits perfectly with the other. When you think of one, it is naturally and automatically associated with the other. This is the mindset you should have with every item on your menu. "What goes with it?" There are two reasons this is so important to better tips.

Reason one: obvious "go withs" are *check* boosters. These particular "go withs" are the ones you **sell**, not give. For example, for a hamburger, a customary "go with" is French fries. If a customer orders the hamburger and does not automatically order the fries, you should ask the question "Would you care for an order of fries with your burger?" (Unless, of course, they are already included, in which case you choose another "go with".) This question serves several purposes.

It shows the customer you are attentive to what they are ordering. They will know you are listening and you are thinking — two very valuable attributes in a server.

The use of the words "an order of" tells them they will be paying for it. If you had merely said "Would you like fries with that?", there is an opportunity for misunderstanding and some customers may believe the fries will be free. The phrase "an order of" dispels any misconception about that.

By the suggestion of the fries, you have increased your opportunity of enlarging your check. A bigger check usually means a bigger tip. (Twenty percent of $8.00 is more than twenty percent of $6.00.) Just don't go too far. Suggestions are smart business, but aggressive persuasion is not. Don't act like a used car salesman. Be receptive to your customers' signals. If they don't appear interested in your suggestions, don't push it. You don't want to annoy them. Being helpful and suggestive is good. Being pushy is very bad.

You should take every item on your menu and imagine several "go withs" for it. Commit them to your memory and offer them at any opportunity to do so.

Reason two: obvious "go withs" are definite *tip* boosters. The "go withs" we are speaking of this time are those you **give**, not sell. Mostly these are condiments and relishes, but they also include napkins, straws, underliners, finger bowls, garnishes, etc. They often include food items themselves. An obvious one of these is the applesauce so frequently served in a small dish or cup with pork dishes. The customers have become accustomed to that applesauce being there. If it isn't, they most certainly notice.

Customers definitely notice your expertise and conscientiousness when you *anticipate* and *provide* the obvious "go withs" *before* they have to be requested. These "go withs" are like pennies from heaven. Scoop them up and put them in the bank!

Think about, and commit to memory, all of the possible "go withs" for every item you serve, whether they are the kind you sell, or the kind you give. Both are extremely important to your tips. Both are quick and easy to implement. "Go withs" — go for it!

Comfort Zone

This is an all-points bulletin to every server, host, hostess, manager, owner, bus person, or supervisor who has ever, or will ever, seat customers. The object of seating is not, contrary to custom or popular restaurant belief, to seat people to the convenience of the establishment, or, its workers. The number one concern, at all times, should be to make the customer as happy and as comfortable as possible. Uncomfortable patrons will usually tip poorly. They will most likely not return frequently. They may, in fact, avoid that restaurant altogether in the future. (I have been known to do so.)

Your customers' comfort is not difficult to accomplish. All it requires is some basic and simple observation. Utilize some split-second mental questions:

Would this person be comfortable in a booth? If so, is the booth large enough for them? (Believe me; not all booths are created equal! Even in the same restaurant!)

Are they a large person who would be hurt by a chair with arms?

Are they fairly short? Would a chair be more comfortable, or perhaps a lower booth seat?

Are they sneezing and hacking? If so, can they be seated somewhat apart from other diners to save them embarrassment, and, protect those other diners?

Do they have a newspaper in hand? If so, don't they need a table big enough to accommodate the paper *and* their dishes?

Is someone wearing a leg cast that would be more comfortable supported by a booth seat rather than having it sticking out from a table?

Are they wearing a sweater even in the summer? If so, shouldn't you avoid sitting them near an air duct?

Are they wearing a hearing aid? Then shouldn't you try to keep them away from the kitchen where machine noises may interfere.

Are there babies?
Elderly?
Children?
Etc.?

Simple observations are easy. Just look at the situation, and picture the ideal setting for that situation. Guiding customers to a place where you believe they will be most comfortable is such a little thing, but so important. Granted, sometimes, it may mean that one server gets a little "bombed", or another loses a table now and then. The bottom line is that *all customers should be investments to future business*. If you don't get them today, you may get them on another day. Learn to help each other for the benefit of everyone. Help a fellow server if they are bombed. It shouldn't happen often. If it does, then something is wrong with the layout of the restaurant. If all of the choice locations are in one server's station, something is mismanaged. Just remember, if your customers have been made as comfortable as possible, *everyone* will eventually benefit.

A general rule of thumb is to seat according to the person in the party with the most apparent possible difficulties. For example: the largest, the oldest, the shortest or tallest, the mother with baby, etc. In short, anyone you observe to perhaps have special needs should take priority. As with nearly everything, this too, has a flip side — and that flip side is verbalization of your observations. Don't do it. Don't say to someone, "Would you like to sit in a booth since you are so short?", or, "I don't think you will fit very well in our booths, so here's a nice table." Grief. That is just plain rude. People with special concerns don't need to have them pointed out or broadcast.

Learning to spot special needs will improve everyone's situation. The happier the customer, the bigger the potential tip, the greater their satisfaction with the restaurant. If you do notice and try to guide the customers to the table you believe would be most comfortable for them and the customer directs you somewhere else, don't despair. Smile. Reply, "Certainly"; and then do as they ask. You'll not always be able to hit the nail on the head; it only matters that you try. You will succeed most of the time.

If you as a server, don't get the opportunity to actually do any seating, be sure to communicate your feelings, and your customers' feelings, to the host, hostess, or whomever actually does the seating. Everyone in a restaurant should be a team and you should be able to pleasantly communicate with your team members.

Even if you haven't been involved in the seating, there are often times when you can improve the comfort of your customer with a little effort. Here is an example.

When I attend a tradeshow in Chicago, I often eat at one particular restaurant. The first time I was there I mentioned that the booth seats were so high my feet wouldn't touch the floor. Dangling legs are uncomfortable. Swinging legs swell and fall asleep. The server employed terrific "I Spy" tactics, and picked up on what I said. He brought me a child's booster seat, and placed it upside down on the floor under the table, in effect, creating a footstool for me. This is not a particularly upscale restaurant where you might expect that footstools may already exist. But that didn't stop this server from making me more comfortable. I asked for his station every time I dined there from that point on. And, frankly, I returned more because of the treatment I received than for the quality or taste of the food. Comfort is essential to good tips. Spotting a special need, and then addressing it discreetly, is a quick and easy way to improve the customer's experience, and, your tips.

Your Majesty

I have often been stunned and dismayed to hear recommendations that a server should try to "size up" the customer to improve their tips. This involves reading a book by its cover. What a deplorable act. This frightening advice has often been repeated among old war-horse servers and managers, and immortalized in server "how-to" books. "Sizing up" a customer in this manner is just plain stupid. One suggestion is that if they "look like high-rollers, try to steer them into expensive items on the menu; if they look like they are on a budget, talk up cheap ones". Another blusters that "women are so demanding". One school of thought says "drinkers are better tippers". There are many references such as these. I am appalled at this advice. My belief is that to follow this advice is to invite doom . I base this belief on both personal server experience and my extensive time spent as a customer.

Case in point. Years ago, I was waiting tables in a higher-end steak house. Most of the servers worked no more than a few hours a day and made great money. One night, a grungy-looking man came in alone. He was seated in someone else's station. The server assigned to that station was so disgusted by the man's appearance that she tried to get someone, anyone, to take the table. I said I would do it. When I approached the table, I observed what appeared to be an older man who was dirty and tired looking. I didn't care. Every person has problems and I thought that maybe he had saved for months for this meal. The manager watched him like a hawk, thinking he might try to run out on the check. He and I got along fine. He didn't smile often, but he was pleasant to me. He ordered basic steak and potato fare. No wine. No dessert. When I took him his check, which was fairly substantial, I prayed he could pay for it. Boy, did he pay for it! He not only paid his check, he left me what amounted to nearly a 100% tip! He said "I want to thank you for being so nice to me. I know I don't look very appealing right now, but I was hungry and just didn't feel like getting out of this garb before eating." Then he introduced himself. He was a famous actor. He was in town to do a movie and had just come from the set. He was in costume and make-up. No one had recognized him because of his appearance. After he told me, it made sense; and boy, did I then recognize him. What a treat it was!

My co-workers were kicking themselves in their you-know-whats! They made a snap judgment that proved to be completely wrong. Because of it, they lost money. The truth is clear. It is not possible to "size-up" customers in this manner. Appearance often has absolutely no correlation to the ability to pay, or the desire to tip. As a customer, I am a perfect example. I rarely dress up. It's just not me. No make-up and sandals are generally my order of the day. I don't drink, so therefore, I don't order alcohol. But can I pay for a $50.00 meal if I choose to do so? You bet. Am I a good tipper when it's earned? You bet! Prejudging is harmful — in food service or in life. Don't do it. Treat everyone like royalty. (Just the way *you* would like to be treated.) Everyone in your station is a King, a Queen, a Prince, or Princess. It costs you nothing but the act of helpful courtesy. So little to invest. So great the reward. The ability to treat your customers royally is at your fingertips. Don't make it second nature; make it your nature period. Be sincerely kind and solicitous to your customers. It's a big tip booster. It's a big spirit booster. It feels great and it works great.

With This Ring I Thee Wed

A server's presentation can be affected by the performance of others — from the host, to the manager, to the chef. But the most closely-related performance to your own, is that of your busperson. All workers in a restaurant are a team, but the relationship between you and your busperson is more than just teamwork; it is a marriage! Your relationship should be like that of the married couple who knows each other so well they can complete each other's sentences. Unlike the host, manager, or chef, the busperson is just as visible to your customers as you are. Their behavior and abilities immediately reflect on you. Because of this 'image marriage', your busperson's philosophies and performance positively *must* be in sync with your own.

Now, if you work in a restaurant where you bus your own tables, this is less of a problem. You have total control over yourself, therefore you control your own image — whether in the function of server or busperson. But you don't have total control over any other human being. Therefore, the key to snapping up the fatter tips which are of benefit to both you and your busperson, is communication. All happily married couples share the comfort of complete communication. You must do the same. You must talk at length with your busperson. Explain what is expected, how you like to work, and how the mutual agenda you both enact will reap greater rewards for both of you. Make everything crystal clear. Is your busperson permitted to help with beverages? Are they expected to monitor all beverages, or just water? Are they prohibited by management from doing certain functions? Do you want them to communicate with your customers? Do they clear from the table during the service, or only after? Do they. . .are they. . .will they. . .should they. . .how. . . ? **Every act must be defined and clarified.** Leave nothing to interpretation or speculation. When one of your customers grabs your passing busperson and asks them for something, how are they to respond? Do you want them to reply, "I'll have your server bring that right away."; or, is it your preference that they say, "I'd be happy to get that for you."? If so, should they then actually provide the requested item without your knowledge?

Don't wait for situations to present themselves to decide on the course of action. Decide in advance. Successful marriages are built on solid foundations of understanding and trust. Your relationship with your busperson should be built on no less of a concrete foundation. Buspeople are important representatives of the restaurant. They can make you look exceptional, or they can drag you into the gutter with them. You are responsible for which way it will be. You are the right hand; they are the left hand. One alone is not as secure as the two together.

A common error made by servers is their view that the busperson is someone beneath them in the restaurant hierarchy. This is simply not true. Each job has value. Don't look down on your buspersons. And don't treat buspersons like slaves. They aren't your slaves. They are your partners. Your busperson is your mate — the Yin to your Yang.

Buspersons must adopt the same strict code of odor-free cleanliness, well-turned, neat appearance, and exquisite presentation, that you must adhere to if you are to make the big tip bucks. If your busperson is seen in your station, or at your tables, (which they undoubtedly will be), they are an extension of you.

I have seen many buspersons whose talent far exceeded the presentation of the server. And yet the server didn't recognize how that busperson saved their bacon — over and over again. Buspersons are an incredible asset and help. Just don't think to dump your own responsibilities onto them. And don't think to blame them for your own inadequacies. You are partners. Think like partners. Act like partners. Your goal is truly the same — bigger tips for the efforts you put forth. Some servers rarely ever talk with their buspersons. How bizarre and how unfortunate for them. Servers who know and understand the crucial impact of their relationship with their busperson know how to nurture that relationship to everyone's advantage.

Communicate with your busperson. Work as partners. Take advantage of this built-in ability to improve your service, and, your tips! You and your busperson can make the 'image marriage' work; and when you do, it will be a tips honeymoon for all!

Butlers — Talk The Talk — Walk The Walk

Your customers are not strangers. Think of them as your employers. Imagine you have been through an extensive and exhaustive application and interview process, and lo and behold, they picked YOU — from *hundreds* of applicants. Aren't you just popping your buttons with pride? They have faith in you! Now picture these employers as famous people — the type who have an attentive entourage surrounding them and whose inner circle of employees knows their every desire. They never have to tell an employee how they would like their tea served to them, or how they wish for their clothes to be pressed, or what type of pens they prefer for signing autographs. Their staff has made it their business to *know* these things — it's *personal*.

Every customer has hired *you* personally. If you adhere to this belief and act like a butler or personal attendant, you will make them fall in love with your abilities. If they love your performance, they will tip more. Make the service as personal as possible. This does not mean infringing on their meal or space. It also does not mean you have to be a mind reader. And it does not mean you must be subservient and act like a slave. (Don't most butlers really rule the roost anyway? They just allow their employers to *think* they are the ones calling the shots! Ha! Fat chance. Butlers are the greatest body of controllers in history!) What it *does* mean, is noticing their particular habits and desires, then accommodating them.

For example, before you refill a beverage, notice where that cup or glass was placed on the table and put it back where you found it. The customer has his dining "space" just as he likes it; he doesn't want to have to realign the components of that space every time you have left the table. Noticing where the glass (or cup or fork) is placed, can give you a clue that indicates a right or left-handed person. Utilize such clues to make their space as convenient as possible. Putting things back where you found them is so simple, but astonishingly, so few servers actually pay this kind of personal attention.

A person who is using "Sweet-n-Low" may not be interested in "Equal", or vice versa. While both are artificial sweeteners, they have distinctive differences. Making certain your customers have enough of their chosen sweetener, is one example of truly personal service.

Extra ice in the beginning? Then make it extra ice throughout.

Lipstick on the cup? Discreetly give them a new one with their coffee refill. (Chances are they will not be reapplying their lipstick until the end of the meal, and now that it's smeared all over the rim of the cup, they probably don't want the world to see it. It draws attention to the fact that it is no longer on their lips!)

Someone's wearing a splotch of gravy? Don't embarrass them by mentioning it; just bring finger bowls (warm water and a slice of lemon) and enough fresh cloths for *everyone* to the table. Don't single out the gravy wearer. If cloths or linen napkins are not available to you, bring a supply of new paper napkins with the fingerbowls, or bring moistened towelettes, or whatever your restaurant stocks for such occasions.

To personalize the service for each customer, you must think like the snootiest, crustiest, most formal old butler you have ever heard of. That crown jewel of a butler would fix the problem without ever drawing attention to himself. He would anticipate his employer's wishes. He would make everyone believe that all things run smoothly — even if the kitchen is in chaos! He would never fail in his duty to be personally available to his employer. Act as this butler would act, and you, too, will make your employer — your customer — proud!

Personally tailored service includes employing sincere "I Spy" tactics to your advantage. Observe, digest, and implement. The way the customer drinks is a clue. The way the customer eats is a clue. The way the customer uses their napkin is a clue. Each customer is truly different. They truly aren't just nameless faces on a food service assembly line. Accept that you can, and *must*, give personal attention to each. When you do, you can say **"Hello Big Money!"**

Chapter Eight

DEEP BOTTOM

Leader of the Pack

I have just enough time for one more story. (Hey — no sighs of relief!) This one is short but may perhaps be the most important tale I've told you. It's subject matter could make, or break, your bottom line.

Growing up, horses were an enormous part of my life. (At least until I discovered boys.) Every weekend was spent at one horse show or another. I won many of the competitions I entered, and I owe those prizes to a horse show philosophy instilled in me by my dad. He told me, **"If you want to win, you have to get out where the judge can see you; don't run with the pack."** I listened to that advice and stayed away from my competitors in the ring. It worked. I have never forgotten those words. They apply to absolutely every aspect of our lives. They especially apply to *you* and your food service job. If you want to win the prize — spectacular tips — you, too, must stand out from the crowd! Many servers will never improve and you can use that to your delighted advantage. If the pack is ordinary, you will look all the more extraordinary! Your customers *will* respond.

It's a short and simple message, but adopting this philosophy as your own will change your tips, and, your life. Be the leader of the pack. Be the best server that ever was!

Smack Dab Bottom

Well, we've arrived at the bottom of the bottom line. The nutshell. We've talked about the do's and don'ts that are so very important to your customers — those behaviors that appall and those that delight and impress. We've talked about record keeping and quick ways to make tips bloom. And we've talked about beliefs and caring enough to help yourself. There's little left to say except to remind you to utilize what you've read. None of it matters if you don't apply it.

Accepting responsibility for the amount of tips you make arms you with a golden key. Accept responsibility for yourself and your actions, and you will rise above any bad circumstance. I guarantee it!

TIPS

Remember your basic ABC's:

A. Bad behaviors and inability diminishes tips.
B. Good behaviors and concrete ability makes tips grow.
C. Good behaviors and concrete ability added to special *far-above-and-beyond-the-call-of-duty* **actions makes tips soar!**

Study the "Tips Scale" that follows, and never forget it. It's the absolute truth. Ask yourself the questions: "Where am I on this scale? What is my current bottom line?". Keep the picture of the scale in your mind, and then do whatever it takes to get to the top. At the top, your bottom line will always be fantastic money and exhilarating self-satisfaction. You can do it; and when you do, everyone will win!

Tips Scale of Success

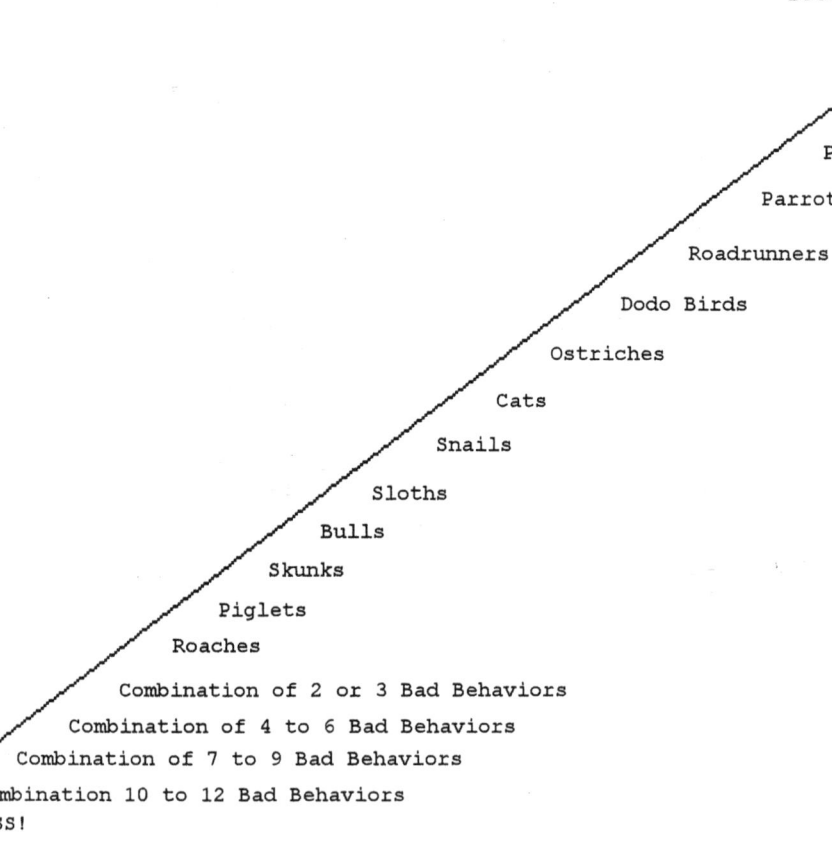

                Combination of 7 to 9 Superior Behaviors
            Combination of 4 to 6 Superior Behaviors
        Combination of 2 or 3 Superior Behaviors
                            Appearance
                        Organization
                    Demeanor
                Quickies
            Rythym
        Listening
    I Spy
ary

    Lambs
e
s

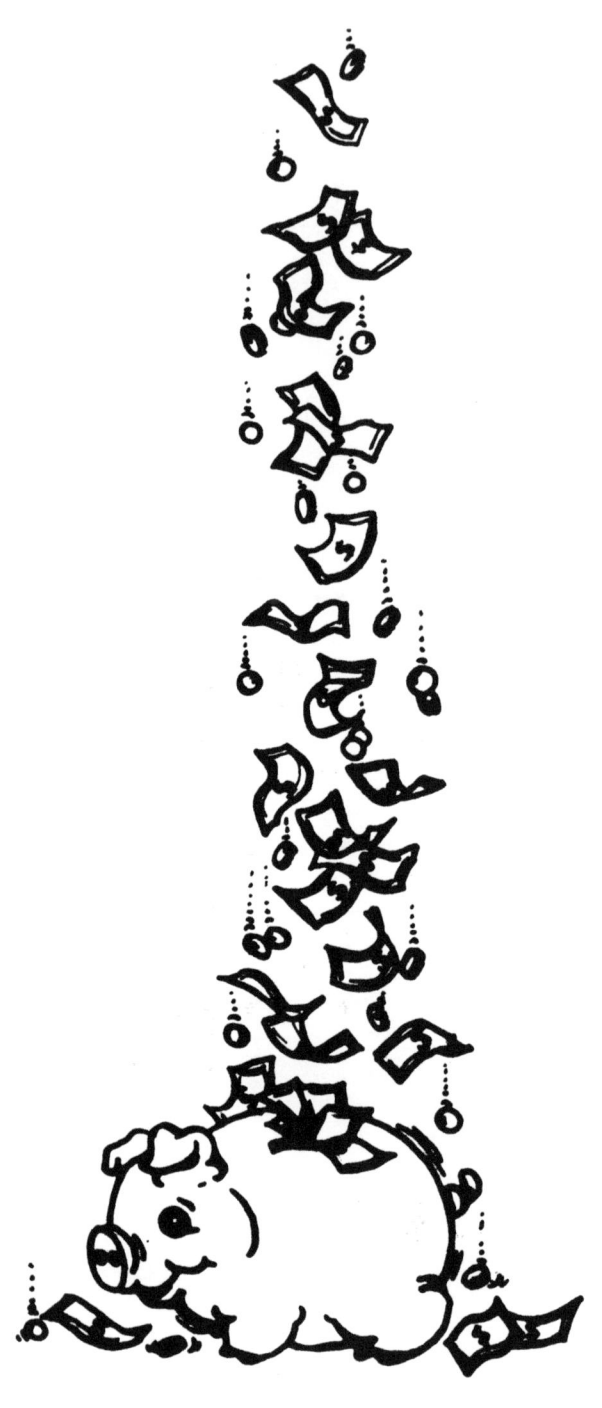

Chapter Nine

FABULOUS ENCORE!

Every brilliant performance deserves an encore. Every brilliant performance is richly rewarded. I salute those of you who have given your all!

Server's Creed

A Daily Morning Affirmation

Now I stand before my mirror
My spirit calm, my mind so clear
I look into my eyes and know
That I alone make my tips grow

Notes

www.ingramcontent.com/pod-product-compliance
Ingram Content Group UK Ltd.
Pitfield, Milton Keynes, MK11 3LW, UK
UKHW041228200426
11947UKWH00034B/364